MANAGING PEOPLE

MANAGING PEOPLE

The Practical Psychology of
—— Interpersonal Skills ——
for Business

ANNE EVANS

Australian Business Library
is an imprint of

Information Australia Group Pty Ltd
45 Flinders Lane
Melbourne, Victoria 3000
Telephone: (03) 654 2800
Facsimile: (03) 650 5261

ISBN 1 86350 007 3

Managing People

Copyright © 1990 Anne Evans

All rights reserved. This publication is copyright and may not be resold or reproduced in any manner (except excerpts thereof for bona fide study purposes in accordance with the Copyright Act) without the prior consent of the Publisher.

Every effort has been made to ensure that this book is free from error or omissions. However, the Publisher, the Editor, or their respective employees or agents, shall not accept responsibility for injury, loss or damage occasioned to any person acting or refraining from action as a result of material in this book whether or not such injury, loss or damage is in any way due to any negligent act or omission, breach of duty or default on the part of the Publisher, the Editor, or their respective employees or agents.

The National Library of Australia
Cataloguing-in-Publication entry

    Evans, Anne
    Managing People: The practical psychology
    of interpersonal skills for business

    Includes Index

    ISBN 1 86350 007 3

    1. Success in business 2. Personnel management
    3. Interpersonal relations I. Title

    650.13

Cover design by Graphic Connection
Printed by Australian Print Group

For IFXS
who taught me a lot.

ACKNOWLEDGEMENTS

My grateful thanks are offered to:

Lorraine Benham, who started it;

Geoff McComas, who enabled it;

Michael Schildberger, who provoked it;

Alan Stokes, who suggested it;

Michael Wilkinson, who said yes to it;

Dianne Douglas, who managed it;

Owen Evans, who read every word of it;

Murray Ainsworth, Jeff Carswell, Sue Harris, Neil Roberts, Yvonne Row, Peter Sheldrake and Cliff Stevens, who commented on it;

Max Lay, Nerida Samson and Peter Stuart, who believed in it;

and the wonderful people I have worked with over a quarter of a century, who contributed to it.

CONTENTS

ABOUT THIS BOOK   1

PART 1. TAKING CHARGE OF YOURSELF

    1   Relationships in Business   5

    2   Who's The Boss?   13

    3   The Time Of Your Life   27

    4   The Big A's   37

PART 2. INTERACTING WITH OTHERS

    5   Careful, They Might Hear You   51

    6   How To Influence People   65

    7   The Power of Questions   75

    8   Lend Me Your Ears   85

PART 3. MAKING IT WORK

    9   Followers Need Leaders   95

    10   The Way That You Say It   103

    11   Change, Development and Growth   115

    12   Building The Team   131

BIBLIOGRAPHY   139

INDEX   143

ABOUT THIS BOOK

This book is about winning in the business world by superb handling of people.

It covers the philosophies and values which are fundamental to the way in which we behave towards others, and offers some help in developing appropriate skills and techniques for handling specific kinds of situations. But the over-riding theme is care - care for yourself and for the others in your life.

Any business consists of four main systems. The first of these is the technical system, which includes everything to do with production. Then there is the social system, the way that people relate to each other in the organisation - including customers and suppliers as well as managers and employees. Thirdly, there is the administrative system, which has to do with the way information flows around the organisation, and lastly the strategic system, which is how power is distributed among the people in the organisation.

Any given problem has its basis in one of these systems, but probably has an effect on all four. The trick is to find out in which system the root cause of the problem is to be found, and to devise a solution which treats it in the context of that system. An administrative fix for a problem in the technical system will not work. A problem in the technical system needs a technical fix, not an administrative, social or strategic one.

The purpose of this book is to examine the social system and to suggest ways of dealing with the problems which arise in it. There are big differences between managing processes and managing people. But a great deal of what goes wrong with the processes is because the people whose job it was to carry the processes out were not managed correctly.

The book is organised into three main sections.

The first section deals with you - how you can take control of your life and prepare yourself for influencing others in a positive, healthy and constructive way. It shows you how to set and attain personal goals in your work and life generally, how to manage your time so that you can achieve everything you want to do and be, and how to handle the factors which cause you stress.

The second section deals with the care of others, whether colleagues, customers or family, and how you can influence the way other people with whom you come into contact feel about you and your organisation.

The third section concentrates on your relationships with subordinate staff and how, by helping them to develop and grow, you benefit your organisation and yourself.

Each section includes a list of further reading which will be helpful to those who wish to pursue particular aspects in greater depth.

I wanted to produce a book which would be easily read by busy managers and supervisors, who might like something to help improve their management of people but do not want anything too heavy to burden their few spare hours. As management books go, it is light reading and I have tried very hard to keep it relevant and free of jargon. Of course I have drawn heavily from my own experience as a manager and as a consultant.

I hope you enjoy the book and find it offers a pleasant, helpful and fairly painless path to achieving your personal potential for a rich, full life.

Anne Evans

PART 1

TAKING CHARGE OF YOURSELF

1

Relationships In Business

Lots of people, when they think about business, conceive it as something pretty impersonal. Huge glass office towers, enormous noisy factories filled with low-paid workers or with robots, accountants carefully going over the sales figures - these are the images of business.

But business is carried out by people. Customers are people, suppliers are people, managers, employees and union representatives are all people. Despite modern technology which enables work which was previously done by human toil to be automated, people remain essential to business.

Individual businesses each have their own particular quality, which is the direct result of the people in it, and which is reflected in the way they behave. Just for fun, I suggest that you walk into one of those glass towers one day and observe the people going in and out. Notice how they are dressed, how they walk, whether they seem energetic or depressed, what they carry, what they say to each other. You will be amazed at what you can deduce about the nature of the business they are in, and how they feel about working in it.

No matter how sophisticated a business' strategic plans are, how good its product, how clever its marketing or how penetrating its distribution, if the people who work in that business are not looked after properly that business will underperform financially.

Lewis Hughes of People in Marketing Pty. Ltd. told me a story about a major building society which spent a large amount of money in advertising campaigns. Lewis asked the staff of the organisation what they thought of their employer's television commercials. The answers he got made it clear that the people serving the customers thought that the ads were dull and boring and lacked any convincing sales message.

The commercials were offering conservative, secure savings and investment products to a middle-aged, middle income target market. But the hiring policy of the organisation was to recruit young, dynamic, risk-taking staff, who were then expected to deliver the promises contained in the commercials, reassuring the customers that their money was safe for their old age. It was a classic case of the personnel policy and the marketing strategy being incompatible.

The solution was not to dismiss immediately any employee less than forty years old. What the managers of the building society did was to involve the employees, especially the ones with direct customer contact, in developing the marketing strategy and in the market analysis which lay behind it. Once the staff understood why the organisation had targeted particular market segments, they were able to modify their approach, and delivered service to the customers in a way that not only increased sales but gave the staff more satisfaction with the organisation.

The standard management textbooks talk about planning, directing, organising, controlling, motivating, etc., in a fairly clinical way. However, with new writers and thinkers studying successful organisations, there is a growing realisation that management is really about helping people to be the best that they can be, and to contribute their talents to the organisation which employs them. Businesses which have high turnover, long production times, mistakes, faults, customer complaints or missed deadlines should examine the way they treat their people.

As a manager or supervisor, managing your relationships with other people, and developing your ability to influence other people, is the most vital business skill you need. Your success in life, in both business and private aspects, ultimately depends on how you deal with the people in it.

It doesn't matter how good you are at your profession or trade, or whatever you were originally employed to do, if your relationships with the other people in your working environment are not functioning properly. Interpersonal skills are the lubricant of any business.

Just as a motor car needs frequent fuelling in order to perform at all, and regular maintenance to perform to the level of its potential, so do interpersonal relationships need the fuel of respect and the maintenance of caring to enable business to be carried out successfully.

PEOPLE ARE COMPLICATED

Dealing successfully with people is the hardest thing any of us ever has to do. It is in the nature of people to be unpredictable; you don't ever have the full information you need to know how best to handle them, you have to cope with your own internal influences such as personal problems, and if you are a manager or a supervisor you generally find yourself taking on board all the ambiguities associated with people issues.

Some specialists have developed the management of people into a manipulative science. Sales techniques and advertising ploys are the result of careful research into how people tick and how they can be influenced to buy certain products. There is nothing wrong with this unless it is being used to take away a person's freedom to make the decision to buy, and normal business ethics ensures that this doesn't occur in most cases. In fact, the same techniques are used to influence behaviour needed to make our society function, such as stopping at red traffic lights, or directing passengers to the correct platform to catch the right train.

You are in a position to influence other people all the time, every day of your life, and you in turn are influenced by other people. Happily, it is possible to learn to exert your influence positively in relation to your objectives, i.e. to achieve the desired results, and to respond constructively to the attempts of others to influence you.

In your job and in your life, there are forces which are brought to bear on you which have an effect on your future. These forces are constantly putting pressure on you, causing you to adjust your own behaviour in response to them. In doing so you exercise judgement and make decisions based on your assessment of the benefits and risks involved in any particular situation. But you are also heavily influenced in your behaviour by internal pressures such as anxiety, fear, indecision, feelings of inadequacy or insecurity and lack of self-confidence.

Let's look at some of the main forces bearing on the life and work of an individual.

Your Superiors

The top managers in your organisation are people you should get to know. They can act as models from whom you can learn how to be a senior executive, a top level professional or an entrepreneur, depending on the kind of organisation you are in. They can also be influenced to help you in your career. For example, they can seek you out for new opportunities, which may carry immediate advancement or may prepare you for later advancement. But you need to influence them in such a way that they notice you for positive reasons and not because you are "sucking up" to them.

Your Boss' Boss

This person is crucial to your career. If your boss decides to promote you, it is often your boss' boss who gives the okay. Therefore you need to be able to influence this person's opinion of you both by your own behaviour and performance and by the behaviour and performance of your boss. In other words, you should be finding ways to make your boss look good to his or her boss.

Your Boss

This is delicate territory. Some bosses are so insecure that they can't bear to have a top-flight subordinate, because they fear they look weak or incompetent by comparison. If you have a boss who has enough confidence and self-esteem to enable you to shine, you are fortunate. Regardless of the kind of boss you have, however, your boss needs to look good and your performance has everything to do with how your boss performs. If your boss is well regarded in the organisation, you are likely to be too.

Your Peers

The other people in your workplace who are your equals, whether they are in your own work group or not, are influential on how you behave and perform, and you are influential on them. The way you treat your peers, and how much help you give them is perceived throughout the organisation and influences the way you are thought of.

Your Family

You are a whole person who comes to work for approximately one-third of the time, not one third of a person who is totally immersed in work. Personal relationships within the family influence your behaviour at work. Personal problems come to work with you and have an effect on how you treat others. Your family life has a greater and more subtle influence on your life as a whole than you might think. It is important that you understand that it can be handled and managed in the same way as your work life.

Your Subordinates

How you treat the people who work directly for and with you has everything to do with their performance, and therefore with your performance. If you give them opportunities to grow and develop their knowledge, skills and ideas, you will enhance your own career prospects many-fold. If you are afraid that they might look better than you, if you therefore fail to give them credit for work well done or new accomplishments, or if you treat them like servants to do your bidding who are not to think for themselves, you are cutting off your own prospects more thoroughly than if you make a mistake which costs your organisation millions of dollars.

Your Subordinates' Subordinates

The same applies here, except that you have to help your subordinates manage their subordinates according to the same principles that you are applying. This is where the concept of an organisation's culture is useful. If you, as the leader of a group of people, develop a philosophy of "how we do things around here", and reinforce that message in everything you do, then that is the culture which will develop and the values expressed in it will be expressed in everyday behaviour by everyone.

Your Network

Networking is the practice of making and using contacts. The purpose of developing and maintaining a network is to give help to others and be able to call upon help yourself in time of need. The power of the network is extraordinary - provided that you have carefully maintained your personal relationships with the people in it, and are regarded yourself as both a potentially useful and a helpful person. Networks take time and effort to maintain but repay the investment again and again.

Your Friends

They help you keep your life in balance. A person totally dedicated to work is out of whack vis-a-vis the rest of the world. To be a successful business person, you need to be a successful "real" person, with interests which bring you into contact with all sorts of different ideas and attitudes. If you stick to one or two kinds of environment you are not allowing your whole self to develop. So you need to cultivate and maintain friendships with all kinds of different people with varying interests.

Your Customers

Everyone has customers. Some people are in sales jobs where their customers are clearly defined, but in reality they have other, less obvious customers. An organisation's customers include the people working in it, its suppliers and its competitors. Employees who have no contact at all with the external customers nevertheless have internal customers within the organisation, and the service they give to those internal customers influences their future with the organisation.

MANAGING THE BUSINESS ENVIRONMENT

As you can see from this brief analysis, a manager has to cope with lots of pressures from different directions, and to be successful must learn to manage them effectively.

In order to make some sense of this complex environment, you have probably developed reflexes which give some coherence to your relationships with people. In many cases these reflexes are appropriate and have the positive effects we desire. But probably all too often you find a situation getting almost intolerable because you have not been able to modify the behaviour of another person in order to achieve the desired result. The tendency is then to blame the other person for being stupid, stubborn or just plain wrong.

In fact it is more likely to be your own fault if someone else is causing you problems. Other people's behaviour is heavily influenced by your own behaviour. It follows that you can change the behaviour of others by modifying your own behaviour.

This means that you must accept the responsibility for everything that happens to you. Instead of blaming someone else for not getting the job done right, you must accept that it may have been your poor communication in not specifying adequately what was wanted, and not checking to make sure you were correctly understood.

A different perspective on the world and your personal place in it is required. This perspective accepts that you are in control of your own future, you can influence what happens to you and how it affects you, and especially that you can influence how others treat you.

FURTHER READING ON RELATIONSHIPS IN BUSINESS

BATTEN, Joe D., *Tough-Minded Management*, AMACOM, New York, 1978.

FULGHUM, Robert, *All I Really Need to Know I Learned in Kindergarten*, Grafton Books, London, 1989.

2

Who's The Boss?

Power is not something you get from anyone else. Your ability to do things is determined by what you allow yourself to do.

The things which are most likely to prevent you from doing what you want are first, fear, and second, preconceived ideas you have about your abilities.

FEAR

Fear is a paralysing influence. If you don't confront fear and deal with it head-on, it can seize you up completely so you never do anything that you haven't done before.

Some people deliberately seek out things to do which involves confronting their fear. It is even possible to be a "fear junkie", hooked on the thrill of doing something fearful, and then revelling in the exhilaration of having conquered the fear. It is somewhat similar to the way that long distance joggers get hooked on the endorphins their bodies produce at the point of pain and exhaustion. Ski jumping, hang gliding, abseiling and public speaking are other examples of situations where feeling the fear is a part of the thrill.

The "fear junkies" have learnt that the only way to deal with their fear is to go out and do whatever it is, regardless of their fear. By not letting their fear take over they are able to expand their universe.

Fear is a perfectly ordinary emotion which all of us experience, and it often has a beneficial effect in keeping us safe. The downside is that, in our desire to be safe, we never venture into the unknown. In fact, this creates a sensation of helplessness and powerlessness which in the end is far more destructive than the fear.

Susan Jeffers has published an excellent, very readable book called "Feel the Fear and Do It Anyway", which should be read by everyone who wants to learn to overcome the fear which grips and disempowers them.

NEGATIVE SELF-PERCEPTIONS

The other major impediment to personal power is what we have learned about ourselves and our own abilities, from earliest infancy to today.

As a child in primary school I had trouble doing sums. My teacher would put big crosses all over my pitiful efforts, then have me stand facing the rest of the class with my exercise book open under my chin so everyone could see her markings, and beat me on the legs with a ruler. The humiliation was worse than the pain. My kind mother spend a lot of time trying to help me understand, and under her gentle tutelage I made some progress, but what I basically learnt was that I wasn't able to handle numerical tasks.

Years later, when I came to study for a Master's degree in business administration, I again found myself incapable of understanding the number-crunching which was an integral part of the course. Graeme, my tutor, was almost beside himself because of my lack of what he considered to be basic knowledge. It took a lot of reprogramming myself to get to a point where I could develop enough competence to pass the exams.

Even today, when I'm confronted with a column of figures which need adding up, I experience the same feelings of blind panic and a sense of utter inability to handle the task, that I felt as a little girl of seven.

TAKING CONTROL

The good thing about both fear and negative self-perceptions is that they are capable of being dealt with, leaving you a stronger and more effective person. Nobody needs to be overpowered by either. It's a matter of mental attitude.

You have the power to take control of your life, to plan your own future and watch it come true. Your potential is truly awe-inspiring.

The first thing you have to do, however, is to accept responsibility for whatever happens to you. If you blame others, their incompetence, their laziness, their politicking, their vendetta against you, their stinginess - you are really saying that these things are outside your control and therefore you can't change them. In fact, for some people there is an emotional payoff for blaming others for things that go wrong - it enables them to escape any responsibility and they can then enjoy the feeling of being hard-done-by and the sympathy they are able to get from others as a result of their complaining.

Once you accept that what happens to you, even disagreeable things which come through the actions of others, is within your control, you will have taken the first and most important step to having a positive influence on the views of those others towards you. Your behaviour directly affects others' behaviour towards you, regardless of whether it is favourable to you or not. So you might as well make it favourable, by in a way that creates positive attitudes towards you.

It can help to play a game with yourself, and behave "as if" you already had the job, status, money, popularity or whatever it is that you crave. Thoughts are like magnets - positive thoughts attract positive results, and negative thoughts attract negative results. By permitting yourself only positive thoughts, and acting them out in your behaviour, you are actually increasing the likelihood of achieving your desires.

Everyone wants to be "successful", but often without further defining the term "success". At a superficial level, success is often taken to refer to all the trappings of wealth such as luxury cars and designer clothes. This is only a rather limited view of success based on the accumulation of wealth. But to many, success is more subtle and more personal. It could be a real success to bring up a fine family of healthy and employable children, to overcome serious injuries following a motor accident, or to help a migrant to become proficient in the English language.

HOW TO PLAN YOUR OWN LIFE

Let's do a bit of Life - Work planning. You will need a pen or pencil and some sheets of paper. The knowledge about yourself which you will gain from doing this exercise will be of real help to you in conquering your fear and correcting your negative self-perceptions.

First, get a pencil and paper and draw a line across the page to represent your life, like this:

BIRTH---DEATH

Don't worry about your life expectancy or try to put any numbers to the lifeline, just draw it as shown.

Now consider where you are at the present time in your life, and put a hash mark # on the lifeline to represent NOW.

BIRTH---------------------#-------------------------------DEATH

Someone in their late teens or early twenties might see themselves as being close to the BIRTH end of the lifeline. A post-war baby boomer like myself probably puts himself or herself somewhere near the middle, possibly marginally closer to the DEATH end of the lifeline.

After you have decided where to put your mark on the lifeline, complete the following statements:

I put the # on the lifeline at this point because ...

I have the following percentage of my life ahead of me: [   ] %

This positioning of yourself in the present is an important step towards planning your life and work. In order to plan your personal growth you need a handle on where you are now, so that you can then work out your immediate, short term, long-term and lifetime goals.

The most useful approach is to try to identify your lifetime goals and then work backwards. This is hard work but well worth the time and effort it will demand, because it will give you an overall direction in which you can then plan your life journey.

Nearly everyone has some over-riding personal values and priorities, but often these are felt sub-consciously and seldom brought to the surface. Bringing these to the conscious level helps you to align your activities with your values.

Here are some values which people often identify as being important in their lives. Please rank them in order of their importance to you personally, allocating 1 to the most important, 2 to the next most important, and so on. If there are other values which are important to you but are not on the list, add them and include them in your ranking.

VALUES	RANKING
Love	( )
Freedom	( )
Happiness	( )
Power	( )

Fame	( )
Security	( )
Wealth	( )
Service	( )
Pleasure	( )
Parenthood	( )
Duty	( )
Expert knowledge	( )
Health	( )

After you have ranked the values, think about what you have learned about yourself from having done the ranking, and write down your answers to the following statements:

I place highest importance on the following values:

These values are important to me but not supremely so:

These values are not very important to me:

Planning involves setting goals or targets for achievement. Many people find the idea of setting goals very off-putting. They feel that life is much too complex to set down in a few written sentences, or they are afraid that having clearly expressed goals will limit their ability to seize opportunities which may be outside their goals but which arise unexpectedly.

In practice, however, we all use short-term goal setting as a technique for achievement in everyday life. Income tax return time is a good example. I don't know a single person who enjoys reviewing all the past 12 months expenditures and filling out forms to help the government decide if you have to pay it any more money.

But nearly everyone determines that they will do it, and set aside time for the purpose, and most of us find that it is not really too arduous or unpleasant, because we have set a clearly focussed goal.

As for limiting you - far from it! Personal goals help you to broaden your horizons, and include things in your life which you would never actually get around to doing otherwise. When a new opportunity arises, your goals help you evaluate whether taking the opportunity helps you along the path to achieving your long-term goals, or indeed whether your goals need revision to reflect the new direction you have glimpsed.

Goals should be clear and written down, but they are not set in concrete. They should be reviewed regularly, both to reinforce them in your memory and to make sure that they are still relevant and reflect your values. Everything you experience changes you slightly, and you need to keep a close watch that your goals suit you as you are now, and not the person you were five years ago.

One sad example of this happening is a common cause of divorce. Husbands who keep developing and changing in their jobs, climbing the corporate ladder, travelling and having new experiences daily, often find that their wives are not growing with them, or are growing in different ways which are not necessarily compatible. After the family no longer needs looking after, the pair are at risk of having nothing in common and diverging values which make their relationship impossible to repair.

Planning and goal setting are difficult mental processes which require time and effort, but it is possible to help the process along, once more by analysing the person you are now.

WHO ARE YOU?

Take ten separate sheets of paper and head each of them with the words "*I AM:*"

Now, on each sheet, write down a statement describing yourself. You will find that you play many different roles in your life, and each of these should be included on one of the sheets.

Some of the roles you identify might include, for example:

- *parent*
- *spouse*
- *friend*
- *employee*
- *boss*
- *youth leader*
- *sportsperson*
- *gardener*
- *craftsperson*
- *entertainer*
- *art lover*
- *film critic*

When you have your ten role statements, go through them and try to visualise what your life would be like without that role, i.e. if you excluded one of the ten roles. Would you still be the same person?

Now rank the ten roles in order of their importance to you, placing the roles that you feel you can least do without at the top and the less essential ones at the bottom.

On each sheet, under the role statement, write down why you have ranked this particular role where you did, answering this question:

I have ranked this role at the top because:

I have ranked this role second because:

and so on to the tenth role.

Now try to write down the answer to this question:

What have I learned about myself so far?

WRITE YOUR OWN OBITUARY

An obituary is an account of someone's life, published immediately after the person's death. It is often published in the form of a eulogy at a funeral, or, if the person was prominent in some way, in the newspapers. In fact the big newspapers have obituaries for newsworthy people all prepared, and regularly updated, in case of sudden death and the need for immediate publication of an obituary.

It may seem a bit macabre, but it can be very fruitful to imagine what the rest of your life will be like, and to write your own obituary.

This exercise invites you to project into the future, to the end of your life (whenever that may be) and write down what you would like people to say that you achieved during your lifetime. Your achievements could include major service to the community, or simply that you were a happy person who brought joy to those around you. It can include anything you like, as long as they are possible and within your power to accomplish.

In preparing your obituary, you may find it helpful to project into the future at five or ten year intervals and imagine what you could be doing. Write down your answers to the following questions:

What will I be doing?

Where will I be?

Who will I be with?

How will I feel?

Then start to write your obituary, beginning:

It is with great regret that we record the death of _____ _____, who passed away last night after a rich, full life. During his/her lifetime, _____ was.. . .

I used the obituary exercise in a career planning seminar for the Year 12 class of a girls' school. The girls thought it was dreadfully difficult to imagine how they would spend their lives - after all, at seventeen years old you think you'll never die! But they persevered and found it a useful technique to sort out their real desires from life from the more superficial ones which are related to fashion or greed.

You will find out quite a lot about yourself from your obituary!

IDENTIFYING LONG-TERM GOALS

Your obituary probably gives you some clues about what you want to accomplish in your whole-of-life period, which is the same as saying your long-term goals. Go over your obituary and write down the long-term goals separately, each one on its own sheet of paper.

Here are some simple rules to help in polishing up your goals:

1. Goals must be expressed simply and state clearly what is to be achieved.

2. Goals must be written down.

3. Goals should be reviewed at least once a year to make sure they are still relevant.

4. Goals must be possible for you to accomplish.

5. Goals must include time frames and deadlines for achievement.

Go through your long-term goals and check that they meet the criteria. Spend time on making sure that your goals are concrete, clear and achievable.

For each long-term goal, work out some goals which are capable of being achieved in a relatively short time frame, which will put you on the path towards achieving it. The rules given above also apply to these shorter-term goals.

Now, for each shorter-term goal, prepare an Action Plan. This should be a list of some small, achievable steps which enable you to make some immediate progress towards accomplishing your short-term goals, which in turn help you towards your long-term goals.

EXAMPLE:

Long Term Goal:

>To become the Personnel Director in a large company (within 10 years).

Short Term Goals:

>1. To obtain a position in a Personnel Department (in the next 12 months).

>2. To obtain a formal qualification in personnel management (in the next three years).

Action Plan:

>1 (a). Prepare a good resume setting out my career goal (in 2 weeks).

>1 (b). Apply for jobs in the personnel field which are within my competence at the present time (on-going).

>2 (a). Research the available courses at educational institutions in my area (by the end of next month).

>2 (b). Seek advice from the Institute of Personnel Management about the best courses (2 weeks after the completion of 2 (a)).

3. Apply for entry to the most suitable courses to start at the first opportunity (within the application period for the course of my choice).

YOU ARE IN CONTROL

The process you have just gone through should have given you the following gains:

- You have identified the important values in your life.
- You have identified some long-term goals.
- You have some shorter-term goals to guide your decisions.
- You have an action plan to guide your immediate future.

What you have accomplished in this process has put you in control of your own life. You are now empowered to do the things which will give you the richest rewards and the greater satisfaction.

These are powerful weapons with which to fight the fear and negative self-perceptions which have hitherto prevented you from achieving your potential.

FURTHER READING ON CONTROLLING YOUR LIFE

DANIELS, Peter, *How To Reach Your Life Goals*, House of Tabor, 1985.

DYER, Wayne W., *Your Erroneous Zones*, Avon Books, New York, 1976.

KARP, H. B., *Personal Power*, American Management Association, New York, 1985.

KIDMAN, Antony, *From Thought to Action*, Biochemical and General Consulting Service, Sydney, 1988.

KIDMAN, Antony, *Tactics for Change*, Biochemical and General Consulting Service, Sydney, 1986.

JEFFERS, Susan, *Feel The Fear and Do It Anyway*, Century Hutchinson Ltd., London, 1987.

ORR, Fred, *How To Succeed At Work*, Unwin Paperbacks, Sydney, 1987.

3

The Time Of Your Life

In order to be a good and effective manager of people, you must be able to manage yourself. Having a working set of long-term and shorter-term goals will start you well on the way to managing others well and winning the corporate battle in the process. Only when you have your own life in order can you devote your precious energy to the task of getting ahead.

But there are still some enemies within you which need dealing with if you are to make maximum use of your capacity and use your potential.

The first enemy is so subtle that it's hard to recognise its presence in your life. You can tell that you have it lurking within you, however, if you ever say, "I just don't have the time to do all the things I'd like to do". For the truth is, you have all the time you can ever use; what you don't have is the skill to organise your time so you can fit in the things that are important to you.

You must take the responsibility for organising your life and your time. By claiming that you have no time you are copping out - and you are stacking the odds even further against achieving what you want in your life. It's very easy to blame lack of time and to rally it as an excuse for not doing something - and some people consider it acceptable to cite time pressures to explain why they couldn't help someone or honour their promises.

But what you are really saying is, " I'm someone who has chosen to have my life out of control, so that I can avoid the responsibility for my own activities". That is the real message which others hear when you plead lack of time.

Whilst writing this book, I was employed in an executive position which I adored, and I spent at least twelve hours a day working at my paid job, because I loved it. My day frequently started with a breakfast meeting at 7.15 am and finished after a work function at night.

I have a husband whom I also adore, who also has a most satisfying job which involves evening teaching. We spend our weekends enjoying each other's company, usually in the country for a change of environment which rests our minds and bodies. We go to the theatre, see friends, learn foreign languages and travel for both business and pleasure.

So when did I get the time to write this book? The answer is: I decided to get up at 5.30 every morning, including weekends, and spend an hour each morning sitting at the computer. My goal was to write something every day, whether it was any good or not. I would average 1000 words a sitting.

Doing things like writing a book is a matter of assigning priority to the task. This is where your personal goals come in. You should use your goals to test whether what you are deciding to do will help you, ever so slightly or indirectly, towards achieving your goals. If it doesn't, then I suggest you decide not to do it, for that reason. You are perfectly justified in your decision for the sole reason that the demand on your time doesn't align with your goals. You don't need to blame lack of time to justify or excuse your decision.

Once you start using your goals to help to identify your priorities for spending your time, you have achieved a degree of power over yourself and others. You have no need for weak excuses such as "no time", because you have the genuine reason that it doesn't fit in your plan.

However, even the things which do fit in your plan are likely to place heavy demands on the time you have available. So you need to examine your life closely and evaluate the way you spend your time in accordance with your personal goals.

I used to think I had no time for lots of things I wanted to do, until I read something which had a profound effect on me. I can't recall where I read it, but it was a statement that "time is the one thing in which everyone is born equal".

Now this is a very revealing concept. The only difference between individuals in respect of the time available to them is in respect of the length of their lives, and even that can be affected by their own decisions. But every soul on this earth has 60 seconds in each minute, 24 hours in each day and 365 days in each year to spend. Some spend their time so as to create maximum value in terms of achieving personal goals. Most of us get involved in all sorts of things which we would rather not be doing, and thus choose to allow ourselves to escape taking the responsibility for our own lives.

The good news is that the management of time is a skill which can be learnt. There are many excellent books and seminars on time management which I urge you to investigate. But in the next section I am going to share with you some of the simple techniques which successful people have used to assert their power over their time and their lives.

PROCRASTINATION

This is the big enemy, and it is first cousin to our other old enemy, Fear. We procrastinate on perfectly simple tasks which are well within our capabilities, and our anxiety level creeps higher the longer we procrastinate, until we are all but paralysed with the thought of the task.

We tend to rationalise procrastination in one of three ways:

I haven't got time to do it now.

I need some information/materials/help before I can start.

I'll wait and see how things turn out before I act.

Let's discuss each of these in a little more detail.

I haven't got time to do it now. This is the standard response of someone who is personally disorganised and hasn't got his or her priorities identified. But it is also used, because it is "acceptable" (which simply means that everyone sympathises with it), to enable the person to conceal the fact that he or she is a loser, always putting off the things which would exhibit successful behaviour, and never getting things done. In other words, it offers an escape from the responsibility of being a successful and achieving person.

I need some information/materials/help before I can start. This is my personal favourite excuse for procrastination. How could I possibly settle down to write this book without making sure my study at home was equipped with every sort of stationery ever invented, polishing up my typing skills, and conducting a full research program on all the available writings on the subject? I put off making a start for eight months by the simple device of getting ready. The hardest thing of all was actually to start, to choose to make the time available and to accept the discipline of writing something every day without fail, even if it was just adding a reference to the reading list.

I'll wait and see how things turn out before I act. This is perhaps the most insidious of them all. When an organisation I worked in ran some courses in personal development for all levels of employees, one of the frequent comments was, "It looks exciting. I'll wait and see what happens before I decide if it has any relevance to me." In other words, people were choosing not to take any action to use their new knowledge, just to sit back and wait for something to happen.

That is something I see in a business environment all the time. People who complain that they are always passed over for promotions are frequently the same ones who never display initiative, never seek additional duties, demand to be paid extra if they are asked to take on anything outside their prescribed duties, and don't research the job they would like to get. They do absolutely nothing to make themselves stand out from the other hopefuls, and then are disappointed because nobody notices or appreciates them.

The fact is that you can choose to put things off and rationalise doing so to yourself and the world very easily. But to get ahead in business, or even to have a reasonably comfortable life, you might choose not to complain, but to take action to deal with whatever you are procrastinating about. The first line of defence against fear and procrastination is action. Five minutes spent devoted to the task will start you on the path to achievement.

GETTING ORGANISED

The keys to getting organised are:

Be sure what you are planning to do is in line with your personal goals.

Break down the big task into small manageable tasks.

Do something.

Be sure what you are planning to do is in line with your personal goals. And I have to add here, make sure also that all your personal goals are being attended to in what you do overall. If you have a personal goal which is based on the value of being of service to others, you could easily find yourself in activities aligned closely with this goal but totally neglecting another of your goals, say learning a foreign language, because you are giving too much time and energy to the first.

This is really another way of copping out. You are choosing to devote yourself to your service goal so that you have a watertight excuse for not attending to your language goal, which is very nice and comfortable if you secretly fear you might fail to achieve it. The irony is, if you don't make a start and commit the effort to learning the language, you certainly will fail to achieve it - and it will be your choice at fault, not the lack of time.

Break down the big task into small manageable tasks. This is precisely the way in which a major project such as building a bridge is handled. The ultimate vision of the bridge is formed in the mind of the designer, communicated and shared with the engineer in charge of the project and the rest of the construction team, then the task is broken down into a myriad tiny steps, all of which, when completed, will result in the realisation of the vision. There is a miraculous quality about it all.

There are lots of similar examples in everyday life. Preparing a meal, for instance, requires several or many small activities which require management and co-ordination, but not all of them have to be done simultaneously. The skill is in deciding the sequence of steps and putting them together to make a whole when they are all done.

Gardening is similar. Again it requires a vision, which the gardener keeps firmly in mind while digging, removing obstacles and generally creating havoc. But after many small steps have been taken, one by one, the garden begins to be a reality.

Why, then, do we find it so difficult to take on activities with which we are not comfortable, have never done before or seem dauntingly large? It gets right back to our old enemy Fear.

And the way to deal with fear is to act.

Do something. I could almost say, do anything, as long as what you do starts you on the path towards what you have set out as personal goals. Action is the antidote to fear. If you are acting, you get involved in what you are doing and forget to seize up.

I talked in Chapter 2 about the value of planning and goal setting in bringing myself to preparing my tax return every year. I have done many things to help myself - I hire an accountant to submit the return, I have a computer system to help me analyse all my income and expenditure, but still I procrastinate on it every year without fail. My problem is fear - I have to overcome a basic fear and therefore dislike of anything involving figures.

But when I finally get out the receipts and cheque books, spread them all out on the dining room table and sort them into piles according to their categories, I find that I am perfectly capable of doing the task. In fact it is not that arduous, once I have got started. All I really have to do is allow action to displace the fear in my mind. After all, the fear is of my own making.

The absence of action, the "wait and see" approach, putting it off as a daily strategy - these are the things which prevent you from getting ahead, both personally and in business. It is far, far better to jump into action and find you have made a mistake - at least you can learn something from mistakes; you can't learn anything from doing nothing.

STRESS

We hear an awful lot about stress these days.

And much of what we hear gives us a feeling that stress is a negative thing that happens to people who are overworked or uncertain about their future, and is by definition a bad thing, to be eliminated.

Nothing could be more wrong.

We need stress to do anything at all, physical, mental or emotional. If you were not stressed, you would fall down, and be unable to get up again.

Furthermore, the thing that makes stress a positive or a negative force in your life and work is your choice of the way you handle it. Once again I return to the theme of this entire book - whatever happens to you is your responsibility and you can take control if you choose to do so.

As in time management, there are many excellent books on the management of stress, and some of these are listed at the end of this chapter. There are also dozens of articles in the daily press, glossy magazines, and features in the health programs on radio.

These will tell you all about the importance of diet and nutrition, exercise, relaxation and a balanced life. Some will take you into the realms of psychology - the power of your mind, meditation and visualisation.

All of these techniques are valuable and worth developing as personal skills to use in your everyday life. They support your choice to make stress a positive force in your life. But they can never work on their own, without your deliberate decision to be assisted by stress and not devastated by it.

What is stress anyway? Many of the writers on the subject give long lists of stress-causing circumstances, health problems, warning signals and dire results, but don't tell you what is meant by stress.

The Complete Oxford Dictionary gives a number of definitions for the term "stress" and notes that it probably was originally a shortened version of "distress". Its first definition is "hardship, straits, adversity, affliction". It is significant, however, that stress is defined as a result of some particular pressure, and not as a state of mind.

I think it is more useful to talk about anxiety rather than stress. Anxiety can be acute (relating to a particular incident or period of time) or chronic (a long-term response applying to life in general). Antony Kidman in "Tactics for Change" distinguishes between fear and anxiety thus: "Fear is the assessment of danger; anxiety is the unpleasant feeling and symptoms evoked when fear is stimulated".

Once again it gets down to how we deal with fear and how we handle external events.

Now don't get me wrong. I am not saying that stress is non-existent or imaginary. Nor am I saying that stress should be ignored and not given way to. What I am saying is that the way we handle the things that happen to us, and the degree to which we take control of our own lives, is central to the way we deal with the things likely to cause stress or anxiety. In other words, treating the symptoms of stress by improvement in diet, physical fitness and ability to relax will help but does not treat the cause of our stress.

Nor does the approach of removing the things which we believe cause our stress - the demand for high performance at work, change in the way our work is done, a difficult boss, feeling cut off from communication, an unhappy marriage - going to treat our stress. The only solution is within ourselves.

By using stress as an explanation of why we are feeling bad, not coping or are unable to perform, you are blaming others for the things that are happening to you, and not accepting that it is within your power to make things different. Your ability to rise in your chosen organisation or profession will be directly influenced by your ability to accept this.

FURTHER READING ON TIME MANAGEMENT

DANIELS, Peter, *How To Reach Your Life Goals,* House of Tabor, 1985.

DYER, Wayne W., *Your Erroneous Zones,* Avon Books, New York, 1976.

KIDMAN, Antony, *From Thought to Action,* Biochemical and General Consulting Service, Sydney, 1988.

KIDMAN, Antony, *Tactics for Change,* Biochemical and General Consulting Service, Sydney, 1986.

LAKEIN, Alan, *How To Get Control of Your Time and Your Life,* David McKay Co., New York, 1973.

ONCKEN, William Jr., *Managing Management Time,* Prentice-Hall of Australia Pty. Ltd.,Sydney, 1984.

ROBERTS, Jean, *Managing Time and Success*, Information Australia, Melbourne, 1987.

4

The Big A's

Anger, Aggression and Assertion are three very strong emotions which need to be managed and used so that negative results are avoided and positive outcomes are achieved.

ANGER AND AGGRESSION

Anger is an emotion we all experience at times, but it is generally a counter-productive response. Anger paralyses you, preventing rational thinking, eliminating options and forcing your conentration on to how you feel, instead of what the situation demands. Learning how to deal with anger is a journey, not a destination, but it is well worth the effort involved.

Anger is usually expressed in aggressive behaviour, both verbal and non-verbal. It often arises from a desire that you be treated by others at all times with fairness and justice, and if you consider that this has not happened, you feel that those who have mistreated you should be punished.

Some people use their anger and aggressive behaviour in the workplace, quite deliberately, as a competitive strategy. By their threatening body language and bullying tactics they are able to frighten other people and therefore get co-operation, willing or unwilling, from them. In effect, these people play on the fear of other people. Some people consider that this behaviour displays leadership and gains the respect of others, and develop a self-perception of strength and toughness, which they mistakenly believe makes them stand out for advancement.

What such people are really doing is displaying their weaknesses. These are people who are so under-confident of their own strength and power to influence that they cut themselves off from all feedback. Is a person working with someone of this type going to offer them feedback on the effects of their behaviour? Most of us would assess the risk as much too high, and simply keep well out of the aggressive person's way unless it is unavoidable. Yet continuous feedback is the single most important thing any person needs in order to change his or her poor interpersonal behaviour, and to learn to substitute new skills.

Aggressive behaviour also generates hostility and creates anger in others. The natural reaction of anyone when confronted with aggression is submissive or passive behaviour, in which you simply do whatever is required of you in order to get it over as quickly and quietly as possible, then put your head back well below the trench line until the next barrage.

But in order to assert your own power, you also do what you can to undermine or sabotage the aggressor, either in the way you speak or by your actions. This attempt at revenge is called "retributive behaviour"; it is aggressive in its own way, and it may be conscious or unconscious.

I once worked in an organisation where there were many professional engineers. Many of these were contemporaries, having attended the same university, entered the organisation together and their careers had broadly level-pegged each other. But as they became more senior and experienced, and as the opportunities as they progressed upwards become fewer, it was inevitable that some were selected to advance ahead of others.

Some of the engineers who were thus passed over had a real struggle with their anger. They were pleased for their colleagues, on the surface, but underneath they were bitterly resentful of the fact that their hard work and loyalty had apparently gone unrecognised. They sometimes got furious with the management, dissipated their energies by feeling strongly resentful of the organisation, and sometimes refused to communicate. The result was, of course, that they reduced their effectiveness in the job they were doing and thus reduced even further their chances of promotion. It was quite appropriate for them to feel disappointed and want things to be different, but this kind of self-defeating behaviour was hardly in their long-term interests.

ASSERTION

Anger is hard to ignore, but it is not hard to learn to control it. Aggressive behaviour is not hard to change, once there is something to substitute for it. The substitute behaviour is known as assertion.

Assertion means simply having the power to say what you mean and ask for what you want, in such a way that nobody thinks any the less of you and nobody gets offended or hurt.

Assertion is about recognising your own needs and wants and deciding to seek to fulfil them, instead of subjugating yourself to others. Very often a mother will sacrifice her own needs for those of husband or child and ends up feeling like a doormat. Or an employee will be afraid to seek better working conditions in case he/she falls foul of the boss and loses his/her job. Assertiveness techniques help us to protect our own rights and feelings and to take a problem-solving approach rather than an accepting and complaining approach to life's challenges.

ASSERTIVENESS TECHNIQUES

You can prevent yourself from ever being hurt or manipulated by anyone if you study and use assertiveness techniques. The principal ones are:

Show respect for yourself and others.

Be honest.

Say what you mean.

Choose your timing.

Adjust your degree of firmness according to the situation.

Don't overdo it.

Show respect for yourself and others. This means treating everyone concerned as a human being, with thoughts, feelings, needs and wants. Try to determine what the other party wants to get out of the issue. But include your own needs and wants in your assessment of what is going on. If you have learned to be easily intimidated or have made a fetish of being "unselfish", you should start very deliberately to decide what it is you want, and then develop strategies to attain your wishes whilst also meeting the other person's wishes.

Be honest. I don't mean be brutally honest at all cost, like telling your colleague that she looks terrible today. In this context honesty means being true to your own needs and the needs of others. Accepting someone else's wants without attending to your own simply fosters the feeling of being hard done by and exploited, which sooner or later will culminate in anger and frustration - both emotions you don't need in your career or your life. You owe it to yourself to express clearly what you want and to discuss it openly with the other person, so you can arrive at a mutually satisfactory conclusion.

Say what you mean. Lots of people have trouble expressing their needs and especially their feelings. Some find it hard to pay a compliment, and some find it even harder to receive one. Expressing affection causes difficulty for some people. Asking directly for something you want is often only just less difficult than refusing someone else's request, especially if it is a request for a personal service such as babysitting.

Assertiveness is about expressing your feelings to others spontaneously and honestly.

Choose your timing. As in selling, timing is important, and so is the right place. If you are having a particularly low day, you may not be able to present your case clearly and discuss it frankly and convincingly. If the other person is preoccupied with something which has a tight deadline, he or she is not likely to pay full attention to the issue.

One day one of my senior staff dropped in to my office and said, with no preamble at all, "I want $2000". I asked what he wanted it for, and was told it was for a consultant to help straighten out a small and specialised filing system, and the consultant needed to start immediately. As far as I was concerned it was terrible timing:

- I was within 2 minutes of going to a luncheon meeting at which I had some important matters to present.
- I had got up at 4 am that morning to drive back from the country and had not eaten since 4.30 am.
- I had just received a request from on high asking me to itemise all use of consultants in the past financial year and to estimate use in the current year.
- I didn't have a clear idea of what was wrong with the present system.
- I didn't know why consultants were needed at all, let alone in such a hurry.
- I wanted to know what benefit in terms of cost saving we would get out of the exercise.

What sort of a response do you think he got from me? (He came back the next day with a case for the expenditure and found me much more sympathetic.)

Adjust your degree of firmness according to the situation. Start with the minimum degree of assertiveness, especially if you are feeling hurt, exploited or annoyed. It is better to play it low key to start with, then you can gradually increase the degree of emphasis. This technique is known as escalation. Don't open with both barrels.

Don't overdo it. Assertiveness is a tool to use when it is required, to help you deal with the situations which cause you to feel annoyance, stress, anger or that you are being pressured into something you don't want to do. You don't have to be assertive in order to deal with every situation; often just listening to the other person is all that is needed to defuse the situation.

If you relate the issue being discussed to your personal goals, you will soon know if what you are contemplating takes you further along the road to achieving them. And if you concentrate on the interests of both parties, especially your own, you will find that many situations resolve themselves. Use your good judgment to decide if you need to become assertive in dealing with any situation.

ADVANCED ASSERTIVENESS TECHNIQUES

There are several techniques which will add significantly to your ability to handle situations assertively and not aggressively:

>   *Being open.*
>
>   *Reflecting.*
>
>   *Defusing anger.*
>
>   *Handling guilt.*

Being open. In order to be assertive in a positive way, it is essential that you are able to disclose information about yourself. Some people have difficulty sharing their inner thoughts and needs, and some even find it hard to talk about what they did at the weekend or on holidays.

Lots of us were trained by our parents to talk about anything other than ourselves, in the name of being polite. We are all familiar with the crashing bore who talks about nothing but himself or herself, and dominates any conversation. But some people also develop a shyness, a reluctance to disclose any personal information at all in case it shows them up as vulnerable, weak or indecisive.

People who are up-and-coming in organisations need to feel comfortable with themselves in order to deal successfully with others. Your personal goals are important here as they allow you to chalk up some small action steps and achievements, and keep you feeling positive, motivated and feeling good about yourself.

The fact is that being open about yourself with others, for instance admitting that you don't know what to do in a given situation and asking for help, simply makes you more credible as a human being. It does not weaken you as a person, nor does it give others an impression that you are weak. In fact the opposite occurs. Those who bluster their way through life, confusing leadership with being all-wise, all-knowing and never off-balance, don't fool anyone. They are regarded as foolish, headstrong tyrants who won't listen to any suggestions and who don't let their people show what they can do.

By always having the solution and telling people rather than asking them, you create a dependence upon yourself and refuse people their right to grow and develop both as workers and as people. You probably complain of high turnover in your workforce. And you probably get it wrong more often than you are willing to admit.

Reflecting. This is a way of handling remarks made to you which tempt you to respond at an emotional level. Instead of doing so, you deliberately try to probe what is really behind the other person's remark, i.e. you seek more information.

For instance, you might say:

> *"So, you feel that..."*
>
> *"Tell me a little bit more about..."*
>
> *"I hear you saying that..."*

Asking reflective questions like these helps you to frame your own response eventually, based on a much clearer idea of what the other person is really saying. It may even make a response from you unnecessary, as the other person may have just needed to let off some steam or, in the process of explaining his or her real meaning, may arrive at a solution without your intervention.

The technique is simply to restate what the other person has said, in your own words or similar words to those used by the other person. By doing this you show the other person that you are interested in what he or she just said and want to know more.

Obviously, to do this you need to listen attentively to what has been said, and pick out what you think is the real message contained in the words. As well as encouraging the disclosure of more information, you are letting the other person know that you are listening and interested in what is being said - balm to the soul! You are also deferring your own response until you are in a position to make one that appropriately addresses the real situation, and not the situation presented at the start of the exchange.

Defusing anger. The worst possible way to deal with another person's anger or violent reaction is to respond with similar anger or violence. All this does is get both parties into an escalating anger spiral which ends at worst in tragedy, at best in a no-win situation with both parties nursing their grievances until the next round, which will be the more intense and bitter for the previous one.

A more positive approach is deliberately to disarm the angry person, by using some simple techniques, including the restating and reflecting approach just described.

First, discipline yourself to respond to the angry person with clear and unemotional language. Pitch your voice a little lower than normal and speak a little more slowly and softly than you usually do. This alone will help to cut the emotional tone of the conversation.

Use questions to define what the issue really is. Very often the anger is not about the subject matter of the exchange, which is merely a trigger for the angry feelings. There is almost always some deeper feeling behind the issue, which usually has to do with the other person's need for feeling recognised, loved, appreciated, wanted or valued. In other words, it is about an aspect of our old enemy, Fear - in this case not yours, but the other person's. Your challenge is to stay cool, probe for the real need behind the surface issue, and frame your response so that it addresses the real need.

As a last resort, you can negotiate to defer the discussion until you are both calmer - but there is a downside to this technique. You risk leaving the other person to brood over the unsatisfactory aspects of life, and although he or she may calm down about the overt issue, the fear and resentment about the underlying needs will continue to grow. It is generally better to tackle the situation as it arises rather than defer it and raise all the bitterness, even unconsciously, in a later, "calmer" discussion.

Handling guilt. Many of us, and perhaps especially women, are brought up to be unselfish, to help others and be useful and pleasant in our lives. And we learn that we should do this at the expense of nurturing ourselves.

Then, when we do assert our own needs, perhaps insisting on some time to ourselves, or saying no when we are asked to do something we really don't want to do, we tend to carry a load of guilt. The guilt can last all our lives - a true albatross! or for just a few moments, but it is potentially hurtful to us if we don't deal with it appropriately.

Unresolved guilt can lead you into a submissive behaviour spiral, in which you feel so guilty that you have to make it up to the other person by acceding to all their requests and putting ourselves out to do things for them. This in turn creates negative, resentful feelings, so that you end up feeling miserable and depressed, which feeds your negative self-perceptions and helps them to come true.

One way in which guilt is manifested is when someone continually apologises for his or her actions, or expresses a view tentatively, as if he or she had no right to be considered.

The best way to deal with your own guilt is to go back to your personal goals, and test your actions against them. Was your action consistent with your goals? Does it help you, however marginally, along the path towards achieving them? If so, your action was legitimate and you can be assured that no guilt can be attached to you for that action.

If not, before letting guilt in, ask yourself if your goals are still a true reflection of your values and needs. If so, you should allow yourself some time to revise your goals and bring them into line with your current thinking.

IT'S YOUR RESPONSIBILITY

The important thing is to accept responsibility for your actions, and to assert your right to do anything that is aligned with your personal goals.

Assertiveness is the difference between coping and controlling. In order to achieve control, you need to understand the other person's point of view and work out what they are really saying, and to focus on what you both want the outcome to be, rather than to deal with the surface situation.

The behaviour many of us learnt in childhood, to play it safe and not expose ourselves to things that would hurt us or get us into trouble, results in submissive behaviour which prevents us from ever expressing a contrary view for which we can be held accountable.

Take back the power you have given others to prevent you from achieving whatever you want in life. Make friends with yourself and get your reinforcement from knowing that you are furthering your personal goals. Nobody can give you power, you already have it - but you can give it away if you think that someone else can make you happy.

FURTHER READING ON ANGER, AGGRESSION AND ASSERTIVENESS

BERNE, Eric, *Games People Play*, Penguin Books, 1966.

DYER, Wayne W., *Your Erroneous Zones*, Avon Books, New York, 1976.

HARRIS, Thomas, *I'm OK - You're OK*, Pan books Ltd, London, 1973.

WOODWARD, Harry, and BUCHHOLZ, Steve, *AFTERSHOCK: Helping People Through Corporate Change*, John Wiley & Sons, Inc., New York, 1987.

PART 2

INTERACTING WITH OTHERS

5

Careful, They Might Hear You

Perhaps as much as 90% of the information we receive is through non-verbal communication.

In an organisation in which I once worked, which was heavily laced with engineers and related professionals, we were often amused by the different perceptions which different people have of any given situation. For example, in a meeting situation, I often couldn't tell you what was actually said, whereas my colleagues could quote individuals almost verbatim. But I knew all about what really went on at the same meeting, by being aware of the group dynamics and reading the non-verbal signals and the body language.

NON-VERBAL SIGNALS

It doesn't matter how carefully we plan a message, if the non-verbals do not match.

Remember the old joke, "Do as I say, not as I do"? All the trite sayings about setting a good example and leading by doing are truer than they are often given credit for. They carry the real message to our public - not what we say. If you don't believe me, just think about politicians, and how easily their credibility is lost if they are caught deviating from party principles in their work or their private lives.

The meta-message - the message behind the message - is what is actually received in the communication process. And because the meta-message is received sub-consciously, it is much more powerful than the overt communication.

Think about the well-worn platitude so often heard in business: "Our people are our most important asset". How often does that sound true and convincing, and how often does it seem like an empty facade? If managers say that their people are so important, why should they be believed if they actually treat their people like slaves, morons or mushrooms (keep them in the dark and feed them manure)? If we say something like "our people are our most important asset", then we must be consistent with it in everything we do.

That goes for customer service as well as management of staff. If we say in our advertising, or in our corporate mission statement, that we are committed to excellent customer service, then we had better make absolutely sure that everyone in the organisation knows how to put that into practice, and that they get rewarded and recognised for doing so. Otherwise customers will question the business' ability to manage its own affairs, because it is making promises it doesn't keep.

Making commitments to staff is fundamental to providing good products and services, and corporate winners know what to promise and how to deliver. While there are a number of skills and techniques which can be learnt, and which enable us to test whether the meta-message is consistent with the overt message, insincerity will be easily detected and will lessen our credibility even more than non-delivery of a promise. If you can't be genuine about such a promise, don't promise.

Non-verbal signals are more than body language. The message is contained in the way you use your eyes, your voice, your face, your gestures and your posture, and the choice of surroundings in which the communication takes place. Such niceties as the way an office is arranged, who sits where at a conference table, clothing and accessories all add up to messages which are subconsciously absorbed and which interfere with the overt communication unless they are totally consistent with it.

EYE CONTACT

Whoever said "the eyes are the windows of the soul" was absolutely right.

Next time you are watching a politician being interviewed on television, make a special point of observing his or her eye movements. How much of the time is spent looking directly at the interviewer? and when the person looks away, what effect does it have? If the person looks down a lot, or away from the interviewer most of the time, does he or she look less sincere, or more? If she or he looks at the interviewer during the asking of a question, but away for the response, what effect does that have on your assessment of his or her truthfulness?

Eye contact is a sensitive issue in Asian countries, where a direct gaze, especially from women, is considered impolite or worse. In most Western countries it is perfectly acceptable, even desirable, to maintain a steady direct gaze with glances away for relief and variety.

In a face to face situation, you get maximum credibility for keeping your eyes engaged with those of the other person, both when speaking yourself and especially when listening to him or her speak. Maintaining eye contact when listening helps you to listen actively (of which more in Chapter 8) and reassures the other person of your attention and the value you place on what is being said.

If you are addressing a group, whether in a meeting around a table or in a lecture type situation, you need to develop a sweeping movement of your eyes, in which you cover the entire audience and bring them all into your gaze, which is in fact your sphere of influence. It can help, if you are addressing a large audience, to fix a point just above the last row of people and return your eyes often to that point, which enables you to have something to look at without actually singling someone out. However I find it most effective to keep your eyes moving around your entire audience.

Don't be reticent about eye contact. It is one of the best things you can do in assertiveness terms, to reinforce what you are saying and to appear strong and sincere.

VOICE

Did you know that your voice changes if you are telling a lie? Or that you can influence the outcome of a discussion simply by the way you use your voice?

Not long ago there was a fashion especially among young people to raise the voice at the end of a sentence. This is technically called the "rising terminal". It is appropriate in a question to use the rising terminal, but the trend was to use it in a simple statement, for example:

"We went horseriding(?)"

The effect of this rising inflection was to make every statement sound like a question, and therefore tentative and insecure. It was engaging in a very young speaker, but when the young started to become established and were interviewed on radio and television about theatre, sport and politics, it just sounded silly and immature. Happily the fad seems to have passed and we hear it less, but there are still some aging young people who have not broken the habit.

Your voice carries messages, regardless of what you are saying. The way you use your voice has everything to do with your credibility and effectiveness.

In a one to one conversation, your voice should be held at normal conversational tone and kept low pitched. However you should work on getting some light and shade into your voice, by using a variety of tone. Nothing is more boring than someone who speaks in a continuous monotone.

In meetings or when speaking to a group, you should raise the volume of your voice to ensure that everyone can hear you without straining. You can never speak too loudly or too slowly when speaking to a packed hall of people.

There are some basic rules worth knowing about the use of voice. A rising inflection denotes a question. A falling inflection denotes a statement. Fast speech suggests impetuousness or impatience. Very slow speech suggests sluggishness or reluctance. A high pitch suggests emotion. A low pitch suggests rationality and logic. A monotonous voice suggests absence of creativity. A very varied voice suggests insincerity.

FACIAL EXPRESSION

Use of smiles, frowns, eyebrows, glances and grimaces all contribute to the way your message is interpreted.

Just for fun, next time someone casually asks how you are, try saying with a bright smile, "just terrible, thanks". If you get the chance, explain, very happily and enthusiastically, the personal tragedy or disaster you have just dealt with. The odds are that the other person will think you are nuts. Your message is not consistent, not congruent with the way you are putting it across.

Your face gives away more than you can control. Poker players know this and wear dark glasses and caps to give them some additional concealment.

PERSONAL PRESENTATION

The way you present yourself by way of dress, manners, possessions and surroundings has an influence on how people receive your communications.

In the British television series "Yes, Prime Minister" there is an episode in which the PM has to appear on television to discuss the government's defence policy. The first decision he is asked to make by his media adviser is to whom he should grant the privilege of conducting the interview. An image, he is told, is immediately created by the choice of interviewer: did the PM wish to appear as a thinker, a man of power, the people's friend or a good fellow?

Then came the next problem: would the PM be wearing his glasses for the interview? With them on, he looked authoritative and commanding. With them off, he looked honest and open. How did he wish to appear? (If he took them off and put them on again during the interview, he would look indecisive.)

Then came the question of his clothes. A dark suit, he was told, represents traditional values. A light suit would look businesslike. (A light jacket with dark waistcoat would look like he had an identity problem.) A tweed suit would suggest the countryside, the environment and so on. A sports jacket would look informal and approachable. The PM's problem was that he felt he was all of these things and he didn't want to *not* look like any of them.

His adviser told him: "If you are all of these things, then you should emphasise the one you are not. Or the one people are in danger of thinking you are not. So if you're changing a lot of things, you want to look reassuring and traditional. Therefore you should have a dark suit and an oak-panelled background and leather books. But if you're not doing anything new, you'd want a light, modern suit and a modern high-tech setting with abstract paintings."

While "Yes Prime Minister" was written for laughs, it contains very sound advice and analysis, in this matter and in others. Your clothes and your personal presentation are more important than you probably think. There are many excellent books on the subject, and there are also special image consultants who are able to help you design the impression you generally give with your clothing.

Dress for men. The dress code in business for men is subtle but very important, perhaps because of its subtlety. It is a language all of its own which tells the people you associate with in business what sort of man you are, the rank you hold in your organisation and the degree to which you can be trusted.

The best course to steer is first, to assess the dress style adopted by the top executives in the organisation, and emulate it, erring on the side of conservatism. The more exposure you have outside the organisation, and the more senior the level of your contacts, the more conservative your clothes should become.

Observe the senior people in the organisation to find out what the unwritten rules are. Such matters as when coats are worn (when going to see the boss? in the staff cafeteria? in the boardroom?), what sort of jewellery is worn, what sort of pens and briefcases people have, or what the smoking conventions are, are small but very important details which tell your superiors, subconsciously, whether you fit in and have a future with the organisation.

Dress for women. Women managers have a difficult task to put together acceptable outfits for business, first because there a fewer role models to observe and emulate, and second, because women often confuse the clothes they love with clothes that are suitable for business.

If there is a very senior woman in your organisation, observe her clothes and follow the lead she gives. You don't have to be a slavish imitator, just pick up the general approach and adapt it to your own style.

As a general rule, your clothes should be a feminine version of the clothing worn by the males in your organisation. Thus if you are in the finance industry you will need very conservative and formal suits to look credible, especially with outside contacts. If you are in advertising, you can have more latitude as the men will probably be quite adventurous in their own clothing.

You are, in effect, wearing costumes, not clothes, to create an image which enhances your prospects for future advancement. Don't make work a place to display the latest fashion trends - the men won't understand and will read your clothing signals according to their own codes. If you stand out as looking too different from the men in your organisation you will be misread.

I know the preceding statement is going to get howls of rage from feminists who would say that women should not be repressed by the dominance of male codes of dress and behaviour. At one level I agree with their views. But this book is about managing people, and dress is a very important and under-rated form of communication in business. Neglect it at your peril! The dress adopted by women in business is, I believe, a major impediment to their advancement if they do not understand this.

As for the men, the more senior your position in an organisation, the more conservative your clothing should become.

Surroundings. In the same way, whether male or female, you need to assess your office environment and read the organisation for its conventions. Family photographs on the desk may be acceptable; your five-year-old's finger paintings may not be. Your office or work station should express professionalism and discipline, and demonstrate a concentration on the job.

Likewise your car, accessories such as a briefcase, your manners and your behaviour should all be deliberately chosen to enhance your image in the environment of your business or industry.

BODY LANGUAGE

One of the most subtle ways in which an overt message can be detected as incongruent with the meta-message is the non-verbal signals transmitted by a person.

Think again of the politician in a television interview. This time look at his or her gestures. Does he touch his nose, rub his eye or scratch his ear? Do these gestures coincide with a verbal statement about something? If so, there is a strong possibility that he is not telling the truth, and his body is reacting to the lie his brain is asking it to tell.

Knowing about body language is important for two reasons. The first is that you can influence the degree to which you are believed, the effectiveness of your sales presentation and the way in which those considering you for advancement regard you, by paying attention to the signals your body sends out. The second is the corollary - you can judge how a person is reacting to you and change your own signals until you get signals from the other person that he or she is ready to agree with you. You can also judge the truth of what the other person is saying. In effect, it's thought-reading.

The study of body language is a new social science, and there is a new awareness of it in the teaching of human relations and interpersonal skills. Good managers of people are aware of their own body language and are able to use that knowledge to help them along the path to success.

Body language is a complex subject, and only a few of the more significant aspects are examined here. Further reading on the subject is suggested at the end of this chapter.

Posture and gait. Your stance and the way you walk send signals about the kind of person you are.

Look at a person you admire as successful, and observe the way he or she moves, sits and stands. Is the posture erect or hunched forward? Does he or she move slowly or briskly? When seated, is the impression relaxed or tense? Try to identify what a successful person looks like when performing these movements. In general, winners stand erect and move quickly, and losers lean forward with hunched shoulders and shuffle along.

Now try to get an idea of how you look when doing these actions. You need to find ways of observing yourself in different postures. You could try out different stances in front of a full length mirror, and try the effect different postures have on both how you look and how you feel. Studying photographs of yourself, especially those taken informally at social gatherings, can give some valuable insights. You could ask a trusted friend or mentor to tell you frankly what signals your body sends out through its posture. Do try different postures in real life - at meetings, in the workplace, walking around the office - and make some observations of how others react to you.

There are two basic ways of positioning your legs and arms, whether standing or sitting, in an informal or formal situation, which affect the way others respond to you very directly. They are referred to as open and closed positions.

Closed positions - crossed legs, folded arms, clasped hands, locked ankles - are giveaway signs that you are not comfortable about the situation you are in, or that you are concealing something. Your feet and hands are used as a barrier to protect yourself from the rest of the world. A skilled reader of body language will capitalise on this message. Even someone untrained will be vaguely aware that something is bothering you.

In a person whom you are trying to persuade, perhaps to make a sale or to negotiate a deal, these gestures mean that he or she is not ready to buy, and you should use questions to probe what is causing the discomfort and change your tactics accordingly. Sooner or later the posture will open up and you will be able to move in to close the sale successfully.

Open positions are the opposite - arms not touching each other, palms visible and legs not forming a barrier. Often the feet will be pointing to a person to whom you are attracted, even if you are looking at and conversing with someone else. (See how subtle it is, and how the knowledge can be of advantage to the astute observer!) If you adopt open postures you are more likely to be believed and trusted.

Gestures. The range of gestures used by the human animal is enormous. Some, like the smile, we appear to have been born with; others we learn from our environment.

It is possible to learn to make gestures entirely consistent with an overt message, but this requires very intensive and special study. Professional actors and confidence tricksters make such a study, and these skills are an important part of their success. But close observation shows that the tiniest micro-gestures still occur to give the game away, even in the most skilled.

Any gesture which covers the mouth or involves the nose is likely to mean that there is an untruth being told or something being concealed. And any gesture which uses the hand to support the head suggests that boredom is setting in. Be careful of your gestures and learn to use them to reinforce, not contradict, what you are saying.

MIRRORING

One of the easiest and most effective ways to establish rapport with someone and to be trusted and liked by the other person is to copy his or her posture and gestures. The technique is known as mirroring, and it is more subtle than you might think.

If you observe two close friends talking together, or a married couple dining together, or two business associates who have established trust in each other, you will notice that they unconsciously adopt the same posture, mirror image with each other. When one changes posture, so will the other one, so that they maintain the mirror position. It is a way of reinforcing the trust and saying to the rest of the world that here is a special relationship.

You can use the mirror technique to help establish your relationships very quickly, without appearing gushy or over enthusiastic. You may feel a bit foolish at first, a bit "monkey see, monkey do", but remember that the other person will not realise what you are doing and will simply feel that you are a person he or she can get on well with.

Just try it next time you are in a face to face situation with someone. Take up a position which mirrors that of the other person. When the other person changes the placement of the hands, say, you wait a few seconds and then change yours to retain the mirror image. The same with legs and feet - you are likely to find that the opening position is crossed (a barrier) and that the position gets more open as the rapport you are establishing by mirroring makes the other person more confident in the relationship.

Mirroring is effective and fun - try it!

How often have you listened to someone saying something and sounding convincing, but you are nevertheless not able to accept what is being said, because somehow it doesn't seem quite right? Ten to one you are absorbing the non-verbal signals and finding them inconsistent with the overt message. The belief and trust you can accord to the speaker is therefore reduced or possibly completely undermined.

Good managers of people need to pay a lot of attention to their personal appearance, their behaviour and their body language, to make sure the non-verbal messages they transmit make a positive contribution to the way they are regarded by others, and do not detract from it.

FURTHER READING ON NON-VERBAL COMMUNICATION

BOTTOMLEY, Maria, *Executive Image: The Essential Guide to Positive Presentation*, Penguin Books Australia Limited, Melbourne, 1988.

CABOT, Tracy, *How To Make A Man Fall In Love With You*, Corgi and Bantam Books, Australia, 1984.

HARRAGAN, Betty Lehan, *Games Mother Never Taught You: Corporate Gamesmanship For Women*, Warner Books, New York, 1977.

MOLLOY, John T., *Dress For Success*, Warner Books, 1975.

MORRIS, Desmond, *Manwatching: A Field Guide To Human Behaviour,* Triad/Panther Books, U.K., 1978.

PEASE, Alan, *Body Language: How To Read Others' Thoughts By Their Gestures,* Camel Publishing Company, Sydney, 1981.

6

How To Influence People

You learnt how to influence others from your earliest childhood. Even as a newborn infant, you knew that if you cried, whichever bodily need required attention would be discovered and attended to. As you grew older, you learnt how to beguile adults, how to play one parent off against the other, how to play on sympathy, use personal charm and generally how to exploit your assets.

But at the same time you were being taught certain things about your relationships with others. Say "please" and "thank you"; use your knife and fork correctly (i.e. as we do); wipe your nose, wash your face and hands before coming to the table; help with the dishes; be polite to the revolting child your parents' visitors have brought into the house.

At the same time, more insidious values were being introduced to you. What will people think if they come and the house is untidy, how much did their new car cost, have we got the same household appliances as the neighbours, always wear clean underwear in case you have an accident and are taken to hospital. Mum and Dad have a fight and Mum gets a migraine; after the fight we go out and buy sweets, or go to the pub; Dad can't stop smoking because he works so hard.

All the things about manners and interpersonal behaviour help us to live in a society, and they serve the excellent purpose of enabling everyone to co-exist more or less harmoniously. But when they become an end in themselves there is a danger that we may lose control. After all, as a responsible adult, what will really happen to you if you don't wash your face before coming to the table, at least once in a while? And if your husband does it, are you angry because he is wrong, or because your need to adhere to the rule is challenged?

It's the same with the illness responses. I learned from my mother that a way to win family arguments was to have a migraine. Then after the argument was safely over, the way to make amends was for the whole family to make toffee in the kitchen. I count myself very fortunate that I found other ways to win arguments with my husband, and have only had one migraine in my life - perhaps I found that the migraine cost me too much and there had to be better ways! And as for the toffee, I have a weight problem which I am very gradually overcoming, and I have learnt that there are other ways than food to smooth over my relationships.

I was taught that dinner had to be on the table when one's husband came home from work at 6 pm, regardless of the fact that I too had been out at work all day. So I was very disconcerted when Owen decreed that he would rather sit down, have a sherry and a chat, and more than likely go out for a meal closer to 8 pm than 6 pm. I had to unlearn one of mother's most sacred principles for a happy marriage.

The world is full of other people, and we can't escape living in it (unless we use the ultimate cop-out of suicide, which is not the subject of this book). But we can take control of how our life is to be lived, and still have harmonious and rewarding relationships with the rest of our world.

I have a friend who is a good example of this. Peter was a very successful entrepreneur and international business man who suffered a heart attack in his late thirties. He was clinically dead for three minutes, and had an out-of-the-body experience which made a great impression on him. After he recovered, he decided to change his lifestyle entirely. He retained an interest in the business but sold the greater part of his share to his partner, who is based in England, and he moved to Perth. He bought a unit on the beach front at Scarborough, where he lives in a very relaxed but not at all affluent way. He rejects the social conventions which were necessary to his life in business, and in his own words, "lets the days slip by". He has unlearned the skills of business and allowed new skills for living to take their place.

There are two key skills which are used and needed in everyday life which enable you to take control of what happens to you. These are assertiveness skills, which have been discussed in chapter 4, and negotiation skills.

NEGOTIATION SKILLS

All of us possess negotiation skills to some degree. Probably buying a house or a car are the most usual times we are aware of actively negotiating something. Those who travel, especially in Asia and the Pacific region, often get a big kick out of bargaining for purchases.

The important thing to know is that every interaction with another person can be thought of as a negotiation. If you are like most other people, you are sometimes disappointed with the outcomes of negotiations in everyday life, whether it is an obvious negotiation like asking for a raise, or something as domestic as asking your son to tidy his room. It is possible to find out what made such negotiations disappointing in their outcomes in the past, and to substitute knowledge and skills which will make the outcomes more favourable to you.

There often seem to be two types of negotiations: the battle of wills and wits, in which at least one of the parties is motivated by a desire to win, and the kind that is really non-combative because at least one of the parties does not want a conflict to continue and therefore is motivated by the need for harmony and agreement. Very often these negotiations do not leave a particularly good taste in the mouth: the winner may not have achieved his or her real goals, and the conceder may feel embittered and exploited despite having reached agreement.

PRINCIPLES OF NEGOTIATION

The best book on negotiating I have come across is "Getting to Yes" by Roger Fisher and William Ury. It describes the method of principled negotiation developed by the Harvard Negotiation Project in the 1970s. I urge everyone who seriously wants to improve his or her negotiation skills to obtain this book. But here the four principles of successful negotiation are outlined.

Separate the people from the problem.

Focus on interests, not positions.

Invent options for mutual gain.

Insist on objective criteria.

Separate the people from the problem. Very often the person you are involved in a negotiation with is someone with whom you deal regularly, sometimes many times in one day. Family members, workmates and tradespeople in your local shopping centre are examples. It is usually more important to maintain the relationship than to win the negotiation.

So the first thing to remember is that the other person is indeed a person, with his or her own emotions, needs and learned responses, and is not necessarily simply out to get you. Most people want to feel good about themselves, and you can handle the negotiation in such a way that both you and the other person achieve your real wishes and at the same time develop further trust and goodwill as a result.

The problem is often that negotiators pay more attention to the matter in hand than to the people needs behind it. I made a casual remark one day that the picture we bought the previous year still hadn't been hung on the wall, and Owen responded angrily because he saw that as a nagging way to tell him that he was lazy. And perhaps he was right, but all I meant was that the picture hadn't yet been hung - I had intended to go on to suggest that we look in the local paper to find someone to come and do it, since we were both so busy.

The trick is to address the people problem before tackling the substance of the negotiation. Is the person tired, irritable about something entirely unrelated to the issue, or really trying to concentrate on something else? Are the circumstances right, is the timing good? Try putting yourself in the shoes of the other person and trying to view the issue from his or her point of view. Try to work out what might be a desirable outcome as far as the other person (not yourself!) is concerned. And then find something to offer the other person if you are asking for any concessions to be made.

For instance, if you are negotiating with your boss to let you take Friday afternoon off, you might try to think what concerns your boss will have as a result of your absence. He or she might be worried about causing a backlog of work, or fear that some sales might be missed if you are not there to deal with customers. Or he or she may have a strong work ethic expressed in a belief that work and the financial security of the family are important values, but leisure is not.

In this case you can prepare for the negotiation by making sure that your work is up to date and that there are others who can cover for your absence if anything occurs. You can offer to ring in during the afternoon, or to leave a phone number where you can be contacted. You can offer to work a longer day on Monday to deal with any backlog which arises, and you could show how your family will benefit from the long weekend away which you have planned.

If you focus on the other person's needs, wants and fears, you are in a much stronger position than if you go straight in to tackle the issue of the negotiation. And you will continue to build up the trust and confidence in your relationship with that person which will make subsequent negotiations easier.

Focus on interests, not positions. Having planned to deal with the people problem, then address the issue itself in the context of what is in the interests of both parties to the negotiation. Too often, someone in a negotiation will say something like , "give me Friday afternoon off or else I'll resign", and then find that the bluff is called, leaving him or her in a position of carrying out the threat or losing credibility. It is far better to look at what is in the interest of both sides in the negotiation, and base your presentation on them.

The best way to find out what the interests of the other party are is to ask lots of questions, open-ended ones which look for an answer beyond "Yes" and "No". Before asking the other person why he or she is taking a particular line, ask yourself that same question. You may start to see the matter from the other person's viewpoint, without it being so obvious what you are doing. "Why?" is a good question to ask when the other person is taking up a position on any issue.

For instance, if your boss reacts very negatively to your proposal that you take Friday afternoon off, you could ask why, in such a way that it is clear you are not challenging his or her view, but trying to clarify the needs, hopes or fears that underlie the position. "What's your basic concern, boss, about what might happen while I'm not here?"

Remember that there will be more than one interest - the boss may be concerned about direct loss of profits, about leaving less experienced staff unsupervised, about a possible decline in your motivation in the job, or all three. You need to bring the other person's interests to the surface and examine them to find interests you have in common, which then becomes your ground for reaching an agreement.

The purpose of any negotiation you get involved in is to serve your interests. To achieve that, you need to be clear and open about your own interests, and concerned to discover the interests of the other side. Your goal is to reach agreement, not to win over the other person. By focussing on your mutual interests, you will be able to agree while still maintaining your relationship.

Invent options for mutual gain. The more options you have, the more likely you are to reach agreement.

The mere discussion of an unattractive option, deciding together that it is not suitable and agreeing to discard it, is an act of agreement with the other party to the negotiation, and builds your relationship at the same time.

How often do we hear on the news that "talks broke down last night and failed to resolve the strike ..."? In nearly every case the talks broke down either because one party, believing it had the correct solution, defended it to the death and failed to develop other options, or because there were not enough options on the table to keep the discussions open.

In the airline pilots' strike of 1989 the whole country was brought to a halt for several weeks because dialogue between the parties to the dispute was not taking place.

While you are talking, agreement is always possible. When you are not talking, agreement is never possible. The negotiator's skill is to keep the talk going. Having a large number of options to talk about is useful in achieving the continuation of talks.

Most of us become wedded to our own preferred solution to a given situation, and we are sometimes very reluctant either to develop alternatives or to consider alternatives suggested by others. But this approach forces the negotiator into defending a position, and prevents a focus upon the mutual interests of both sides. This is all that is needed to produce a no-win situation, and is death to the prospect of an agreement.

Insist on objective criteria. Instead of sticking to your own doubtless correct but unsubstantiated idea of what the house is worth or what you should pay for the antique coal scuttle, you have a better chance of reaching agreement on the issue if you first reach agreement on the criteria to be used. An independent, objective assessment of the value of whatever you are negotiating about is a great help, and worth paying for if necessary.

Sometimes the objective criteria are quite hard to obtain. Such criteria as market value or going wage rates are relevant and can easily be applied, which frees both parties to the negotiation to concentrate on reaching agreement, rather than get hung up on the amount to be exchanged. In other situations there is more difficulty.

For instance, say you want to change from working full time to working part time, but your employer is uncertain because there is no provision for part time work in the award under which you are employed. You might find that there is a precedent in a competitor's firm, or a really good reason from your employer's point of view (not your own!) which would help him or her to support your desire, or a tradition in a similar kind of work but in a different industry.

As a minimum, whatever you use as an objective criterion should be independent of both parties to the negotiation, and should apply equally to both sides. Fair standards and/or fair procedures, determined and applied outside and prior to the current negotiation, are what you are looking for.

Once found, you then seek agreement to use the objective criteria. You could suggest to the other person that you should both seek the needed criteria and perhaps make it a joint exercise. Once the criteria are agreed, you can then use them to establish the principles of your negotiation, which protects you from succumbing to pressure. You need only refer to the principles thus established to deflect any other arguments.

By following these four basic rules in negotiation, you will be able to handle any issue in such a way that both you and the other person feel good about the result. You will have the power to make things go the way you want them, without damaging your relationships or exploiting anyone.

FURTHER READING ON NEGOTIATING SKILLS

COHEN, Herb, *You Can Negotiate Anything*, Angus and Robertson, Sydney, 1982.

FISHER, Roger, and URY, William, *Getting To Yes*, Hutchinson, London, 1982.

NIERENBERG, Juliet, and ROSS, Irene, *Women and the Art of Negotiating*, Simon and Schuster Inc., New York, 1985.

7

The Power Of Questions

Questions are the most powerful tools you can possibly have. By asking questions rather than attempting to provide answers, you can keep discussion open, tap into the wisdom and insights of others and conceal your own agendas until they are elicited from your confederates.

Corporate winners are never afraid to ask questions. They are not worried about exposing ignorance. Instead, the best and most highly paid management consultants make a practice of asking dumb questions, the questions with obvious answers, the things that are taken for granted. This is where they find the real cost savings, the real pay-dirt.

Questions are your path to real information. They enable you to obtain information from the legitimate source, then to test it in the real world, the world of the user or the customer. A true corporate winner never accepts the word of the people in charge of a function without trying out the concept on those who have a stake in it, in the real world.

In negotiations, questions enable you to determine the real needs of the other party. In leading and motivating people, questions enable you to shape your vision to strike a chord with the people you are depending upon to make the vision come true. And in interpersonal relationships at all levels, questions help you establish rapport and trust.

PURPOSE OF QUESTIONS

Making the other person feel good. There is nothing like demonstrating to the other person that you are truly interested in what he or she has to say, to achieve a degree of rapport. It is not manipulative or deceitful to want the other person to feel that he or she is getting the best result possible out of the interaction you are both in; it is merely proper consideration for the other person. If one party feels defeated or degraded, nobody has really won, because of the negative feeling generated which will be carried forward to future negotiations. So it is worth using questions to make sure the full views of the other side are explored and understood.

Keeping discussion going. Whilst questions are being asked and answered, discussion is kept open and no positions are being put. It is worth deferring offers, positions or decisions until after all efforts to understand the needs of the other person are explored and fully understood. You can use questions to keep discussion positive and focussed on the interests of both parties, and the desired outcome of the discussion or negotiation, rather than on the positions adopted by either side.

Getting information. This is where you can gain a strategic advantage. By the judicious use of questions, you can saturate yourself in the point of view of the other person, so you can prepare a complete case which both satisfies your own needs and meets the other person's needs in such a way that your proposal seems desirable and is readily agreed to.

Clarifying. Questions enable you to probe a situation or a response to make sure you have understood correctly. In doing so you reassure the other person that what he or she has said is important enough to be properly understood.

Asking a question to clarify or amplify what has been said by the other person is a most effective way of both delaying a response on your part and of obtaining more information upon which to base your ultimate response.

Gaining insight. There is always at least one other way of looking at any given problem or situation. By asking questions freely, you reap the benefits of obtaining the perspectives of people with other disciplines, other cultural norms and other points of view, which will improve the quality of your decision making.

Insight is about accepting that your own best thinking on a problem is not the only or the best solution. A product or an idea might be unsaleable to one customer, but extremely valuable to another. For example, you might have difficulty selling water purification treatment to consumers in rural or mountainous areas who take their water directly from pure springs, or who collect rainwater - but you might find real interest from residents of mining communities, industrial areas or large cities.

By bringing the views of different people to bear on a situation, you create the opportunity to reach new solutions involving strategic changes. But only by asking questions can you bring a degree of confidence and trust sufficient to elicit these different, perhaps radical, points of view.

Saturate yourself with information. In other words, prepare yourself thoroughly, both before and during a negotiation or interaction. And the only way to do this completely is by asking lots and lots of questions. Seek information about the issue, its background, how it fits in with current policies, its relevance to the future, and everything else you can think of. Pretend you are a barrister going into court for a trial, with this your one opportunity to make the best case for your client. Or a management consultant hoping to be offered a half-million dollar assignment!

NEGATIVE ASPECTS OF QUESTIONS

Trick questions. It is possible to use questions to trick the other person into an admission or to get your opponents to contradict a previous statement. If you use questions for this purpose, be sure you do so in the full understanding that you are putting the future relationship at risk. By forcing the other side to lose face or credibility you are eliminating any chance of fruitful interaction in the future.

Timing. Your questions should be timely and asked graciously. Questions should start with general issues and gradually focus on specifics. If you get too direct, too soon, you run the risk of putting the other person on guard and creating a defensive attitude rather than the attitude of open communication and mutual problem solving which you are seeking.

The nature of the relationship. Your questions should be framed in such a way as to take into account the relationship you have with the other person. You would normally frame your questions differently with a total stranger from the way you would put them to a close friend. Even if it turns out that the real interests of the other person are indeed personal, your questions should elicit this need without appearing to pry too deeply into personal affairs. Skilful questioning and a genuine interest in the other person will soon bring out what you need to know without your being a nosey parker.

KINDS OF QUESTIONS

Skilled teachers, interviewers and moderators of debates on television are able to use questions in such a way as to keep discussion flowing and wide-ranging. Top salespeople pay great attention to the art of questioning, both to bring out the prospect's needs and to bring the sale to a successful close. Questioning techniques are easy to learn and will repay the small effort involved many times over.

Dumb questions. These are probably the most important questions you will ever ask. They will open up your own thinking and the thinking of those around you, because they will generally be testing the rationale for why things have always been done in a particular way.

Some people are shy of asking questions because they feel it exposes their ignorance. A truly secure person with well-developed self-esteem is never worried about admitting he or she doesn't know something. In fact, asking the question shows that you really care about understanding what is being said, and reassures the other person that you are indeed listening and processing the information.

Examples of dumb questions which are really smart to ask are:

> *"What does that word mean?"*
>
> *"Why does it go there?"*
>
> *"Who has to sign it? Why at that level?"*
>
> *"I don't quite follow.
> Could you go over it again please?"*

Open-ended questions. These are the questions which keep the discussion open, allowing you to probe for the real issues and needs behind the matter in hand. They are your most faithful tools of trade and, properly used, will reveal a treasure trove of information.

Open-ended questions are the ones which don't permit a simple yes or no answer. They are asked in such a way that the reply must be expressed in terms of explanation, fact or personal opinion. The key to asking open-ended questions is the use of Kipling's "Six Honest Serving Men" : What, Why, When, How, Where and Who. Examples are:

> *"What do you think about...?"*
>
> *"How could we improve...?"*
>
> *"When could we do...?"*

Open-ended questions are very good to get people thinking about what they do and how they do it, and to get them participating in making changes and improvements.

Yes - No questions. These are designed to obtain the opposite response from open-ended questions. They tend to be used in formal interrogations such as in court, where the questioner is trying to elicit fact but is also trying to eliminate opinion. Because they are designed for this, they are not good for helping people to feel involved and to get them participating in discussion. Open-ended questions should be used for that purpose.

Yes - No questions elicit yes or no answers. If you were hoping to get an open response, but phrase your question in a yes - no way, you are likely not to get the information you were seeking, especially if the other person doesn't trust you and wants to keep his or her opinions private.

For example, suppose one of your staff is working less well than usual and you think there might be a personal problem affecting her. You go up and say, "I'm concerned about you, is there anything wrong at home?" If your associate wants to discuss her personal situation she might respond to the implied invitation, but she's more likely to say "No, no problems at all," even if it's not true. You are then in the position that you are still worried about her fall-off of performance but you can't open discussions again without appearing prying.

Another way to approach the issue would be to say to her, "Look, your work isn't as good as it usually is. What is the reason for the fall-off?" By asking an open-ended question and focussing on the matter in which you both have an interest, you are able to probe the situation and the personal problem will most likely be aired on your associate's initiative rather than yours.

Yes - No questions do have their place, however. You might use them in a sales presentation, for instance, where you ask them in order to obtain a pattern of agreement with the benefits you are suggesting. Just don't use them for fact-finding.

Reflective questions. These are used to restate or reflect back to the other person that you have heard and understood what has been said, and to invite the disclosure of additional information:

> *"So, you feel that...?"*
>
> *"Are you saying that...?"*

Reflective questions should not contain any judgment or evaluation on your part; their purpose is simply to generate trust in the exchange by reassuring the other person that you have accepted their statement in its own right and have received its content as it was intended.

Leading questions. Another legal technique, not regarded as playing quite fair. The question is framed in such a way as to elicit the desired answer:

> *"Don't you think that...?"*

This question should be used very sparingly, if ever. It doesn't help to generate open communication of ideas, and creates an atmosphere of distrust.

Rhetorical questions. These are questions asked for effect, and to which you do not expect an answer, unless you provide it yourself.

> *"Have you ever wondered how to breed guinea pigs?"*

The technique is sometimes used in public speaking to emphasise a point, but it is rarely appropriate in ordinary communication.

Directive questions. These are questions which you can use to focus on a desired outcome. Salespeople use directive questions to bring the prospect closer to the buying decision:

> *"So, you agree that...?"*

Questions are your best means of developing knowledge about your workplace, your people and your customers. Every player in the corporate game needs to understand the value of questioning techniques and to learn to use them to advantage.

The higher you climb in your organisation, the more people will come to you with their questions, expecting answers. And the higher your level in the hierarchy, the fewer answers you should give, and the more questions you should ask.

FURTHER READING ON THE ART OF QUESTIONING

HAWKINS, Leo, and HUDSON, Michael, *Effective Negotiation*, Information Australia, Melbourne, 1986.

HICKMAN, Craig R., and SILVA, Michael A., *Creating Excellence*, Unwin Paperbacks, London, 1985.

NIERENBERG, Juliet, AND ROSS, Irene S., *Women and the Art of Negotiating*, Simon and Schuster, New York, 1985.

PETERS, Tom, *Thriving on Chaos: Handbook for a Management Revolution*, Macmillan, London, 1987.

8

Lend Me Your Ears

Listening means taking people seriously. It has to do with respect for the other person, a genuine desire to hear his or her ideas, and a real wish to communicate.

It is widely recognised that communication is a two-way process. But how many of us really strive to make it so? All too often I hear of incidents where someone has identified a lack of communication as part of a crisis situation, and the cry goes up, "they have been told often enough..." But what has the teller done to make sure the message was received?

It is the clear responsibility of the sender of the message to ensure that the message has been received by the intended recipients, is clearly understood and is being applied. It is not OK to blame the communication process for failure, nor to blame the intended recipient of the message for failed communication.

The only way that the sender of the message can confirm that the message has been received and understood is by constant testing. And the only way to do that is to go out there and ask, and listen.

Listening achieves more than confirming the efficacy of the communications system. It allows you to tap into the greatest and richest source of knowledgeable advice to which you could possibly have access: the collective wisdom of the people who know most about the work being done. Listening to the people on the front line tells you how your customers can be served better, how your costs can be reduced and how your processes can be streamlined to make the job easier, more satisfying and more profitable.

All that is needed to loosen this tremendous resource is your two ears.

So what keeps you in your office and insulated from the real people doing the real work? Or from the real customers out there who can tell you what's wrong with your product or service?

More than likely it's our old enemy, Fear.

Nobody, especially a newly promoted supervisor or middle manager, likes to think that there may be people among your subordinates who are more knowledgeable than you are. Your position is tenuous enough without exposing yourself to the idea that you may have among your associates someone who is cleverer than you, thus being a potential threat or rival, and heaven forbid that someone below you in the hierarchy is right while you are wrong. After all, you're paid to know the right answers, right? Wrong!

This sort of attitude cuts you off, permanently if you are not careful, from the most important resources you have - the knowledge of your staff, the reactions of your customers. And everyone has customers - the personnel department's customers are the employees and the management of the organisation; the accounting department's customers are the operating departments of the organisation. If you don't deal with outside customers directly, then you certainly deal with internal customers. Listen to them!

To do so effectively, you have to engage yourself in the listening process. Waiting for people to tell you things is not enough. You need to go out and seek out the people who really know what is going on, what could be done better, cheaper and more effectively, find out their opinions and take action to get them implemented.

Find ways to connect with the organisation at all levels. It is no good speaking only to your immediate subordinates - they have a sheltered perspective on things, and also have a vested interest in keeping you happy and out of their way. You need to go direct to the people doing the job, serving the customer, delivering the goods.

Better still, go out and work on the counter, spend a day or so in the delivery vehicle, talk to the suppliers. And all the time, engage in active listening which keeps the information coming and enables you to probe what is really going on.

LISTENING TECHNIQUES

Take all the time it needs. Listening properly takes time, and I don't care what your job is, listening is your job if you are a manager of people. If someone is just starting to tell you what things are really like, you will generate distrust and bad feelings, as well as depriving yourself or the information, if you cut the session short. If you absolutely must go, like because you have to collect your child from the creche, make another time with the person to continue the discussion. If you do this, you will need to make an extra effort at the beginning of the next meeting, to recreate the atmosphere in which the information was initially forthcoming.

Treat the other person with respect. This means not judging, not ridiculing and not defending, but accepting the other person's point of view at face value, for what it is. It takes discipline. It takes a real, genuine attitude of wanting to know, rather than wanting to be reinforced in your own fantasy of how things are. Listen carefully and ask more questions - it's gold you're mining.

Shut up and listen - don't frame your response. Brain speed works at about 90 times the rate of the speed of speech. So it is likely that your mind will soar ahead of what you are hearing and will naturally tend to start working on your defence of what is being said. Stop it. Use the free brain space instead to link back to what this person has said on an earlier occasion, or what someone else said on the same or a related topic. Use the time to frame more questions. On no account let your attention wander from what is being said now - if you do, you may forfeit the privilege of ever hearing it again, because you are likely to sacrifice the other person's tentative and tremulous trust in you which has been given for this moment only.

Pay attention. I can't say it too often. Let the other person see that you have only one thing on your mind at this moment, and that is what he or she has to say. The greater the difference in rank between you, the more significant the moment is to both of you. Give your whole mind to this communication. Afterwards, let the person see that you really were listening, by taking whatever action is necessary to remove the bottleneck or simplify the procedure which you learnt about in the discussion.

Take notes. One way to ensure that you engage your mind in what you are hearing is to write it down. The more details you seek, the less reliable is your memory. Write it down, and at the very least you let the other person know that you are sufficiently interested in what is being said to record the material for future consideration. And having written it, do take it further!

Listen for key words and key emotions. These give you the clue to further exploration. Keep an ear open for the feelings behind the words. You will very likely find that the frustration someone is expressing with a process is based on a procedure which was established twenty-five years ago and which has no bearing on the situation today.

Rephrase, restate. You tell a person that you value what he or she is telling you, and obtain more information than you might otherwise get, by reflecting what has just been said back to the speaker.

"If I have understood you correctly, you feel that..."

All you have to do is to suspend judgement and concentrate on understanding the other person's point of view. Understanding does not imply acceptance. It merely enables a degree of trust to develop which will facilitate the ultimate agreement on a solution. It is not a sign of strength or of leadership to neglect or diminish the other person's point of view - quite the opposite.

Ask for repetition, clarification, amplification, examples. Make sure you grasp completely what you are being told. Seek real life "for instance" anecdotes. Find out the concrete facts behind the impressions you are being given. The more senior the person you are speaking with, the more insistent you should be on obtaining concrete examples. As a general rule, the higher up the hierarchy, the less detailed the knowledge and the more likely the room for error in the information.

Give unspoken feedback - eye contact, nods, smiles. It is important to let the other person know that you are still listening. Rather than punctuate the information with comments, advice or criticism, keep the non-verbal encouragement going.

Don't criticise, evaluate, comment or pass judgement. The time for you to show your masterly command of the situation will come later. Don't waste the opportunity to find gold by interfering with its appearance. Use the time you have to listen to your informant and to seek as much additional information as you can. Later, in the silence of your lonely room, you can evaluate it and link it to other data. And in checking your information, never reveal the source of your knowledge; if you do, you don't deserve to hear any more, and you probably won't.

Keep your mind open. How many times do I have to say it? Don't judge. Don't shut out unpalatable information. It is always possible that the other person is right and you are wrong, even if you earn twenty times the other person's salary. Check and recheck before you dismiss someone's opinion, especially if the someone is actually doing the job in question.

Don't jump to conclusions. Let your mind play on the information it is receiving and save the processing for later. Your energy is better used in testing out the information, seeking ever more detailed explanations and concrete examples, and in particular seeking your informant's ideas of what can be done to fix or improve the situation. Don't fall into the trap of being the all-knowing boss.

Hear it all - don't engage in wishful hearing. Above all, let the information sink in without filtering it to suit your own construct of reality. Too often we hear only what we want to hear - and seeing that, our staff tell us only what they think we wish to hear. This acts as a double filter which has a deadly insulating effect upon our perceptions. Keep relentlessly sacrificing your own wishes of how it ought to be, and concentrate on exposing the reality.

"Observe the organisation with your ears" is a maxim of Ian Stoney, Chief Executive of the Roads Corporation of Victoria. He is a past master at finding things out. Any of his senior managers will tell you that they are amazed at the depth and detail of his information, and he never divulges his sources. He keeps his senior people on their toes by being in constant touch with the people who are doing the work.

Listening means integrity and sincerity and if you don't mean it, don't do it. If you spend a lot of time going around engaging people in conversation, but then nothing happens, you lose all credibility in the process, if not in yourself as a leader.

FURTHER READING ON THE ART OF LISTENING

NIERENBERG, Juliet, and ROSS, Irene S., *Women and the Art of Negotiating,* Simon and Schuster, New York, 1985.

PETERS, Tom, *Thriving on Chaos: Handbook for a Management Revolution,* Macmillan, London, 1987.

PETERS, Tom, and AUSTIN, Nancy, *A Passion For Excellence,* Collins, London, 1985.

WATERMAN, Robert H., *The Renewal Factor,* Bantam Books, New York, 1987.

PART 3

MAKING IT WORK

9

Followers Need Leaders

Those of you who are Gilbert and Sullivan fans may have seen, on stage or on television, Jonathan Miller's production of the opera "The Mikado", in modern dress and set as a parody of comedy and musicals of the 1920s and 1930s.

It takes courage to set aside as proud a tradition as the d'Oyley Carte set pieces, but Miller showed enormous leadership in physically demonstrating to the players, each a recognised artist in his or her own right, just how he wanted the piece performed, and getting their understanding and agreement to the desired style. It is a masterly demonstration of managing people, leading them to exert their skills in a particular direction which had not previously occurred to them, but which they became motivated to bring to reality.

MOTIVATION

There is a lot of nonsense talked about motivation. I once worked in an organisation where the Workshops Manager came to me for help in how to motivate the workforce. He had great trouble in believing that the people in the workshops were anything other than simple organisms, responding in a simplistic approach to motivating forces, such as more money.

In fact, it is not possible to motivate people. People are motivated. If you don't believe me, just look at the behaviour of people at 5 pm on a Friday evening - they are motivated then, all right - to get out the door and on to what they have planned for the weekend.

The challenge for a manager is to find out what motivates the people and to use it for the advantage of both the employees and the organisation. More often than not, the employees will be motivated by their wish to do a good job, to have pride in saying which organisation they work for, and in having a say and being able to contribute their ideas about how to do the job better.

This makes the job of the manager both easier and more difficult. The corporate winner is able to articulate the overall vision for the organisation, the product, service or process in question, and then to be infinitely flexible and negotiable as to the how.

ESSENTIALS OF LEADERSHIP

Developing a vision. This is the first, the primary duty of the leader. It requires the leader to think through exactly what the organisation or department should be like in one, two or five years from now, and develop the concept in detail, then to articulate it with clarity.

In one organisation I was the head of a unit which provided career information materials to schools and employment services, in written, audio and video forms. Les, one of the managers in this group, who was in charge of the production and distribution of a major product, had what I considered to be unrealistically grandiose plans for the product. It was a highly bureaucratised organisation and I was concerned at the time to preserve my own status as a manager. In order to achieve this and keep the good opinion of my superiors, I kept Les firmly under control, much to my shame, never letting his big ideas do more than break the surface, and quickly beating them down out of sight again. I did not have a vision of my own for the product, and so was unable to come to grips with anyone else with a vision.

Having a vision is not about having pipedreams or thinking big for its own sake. It is a very simple extension of the kind of planning which was discussed in Part 1 of this book. It is about identifying strengths and weaknesses, planning to capitalise on the first and minimising the second, and then using the goals as a means of always testing whether you are still heading to where you want to go.

The vision for your work is intrinsically the same as your personal goals. The main difference is that to achieve your personal goals, often only you need to know what the goals are and when you have achieved them. In an organisation, your goals, or vision, must be shared with your workmates, especially your subordinates, so you can all work collectively towards the achievement of them.

Sharing the vision. In order to share the vision, you need to be very clear about it yourself. Perhaps, rather than developing the vision as a grand plan which you then reveal to your grateful and admiring colleagues, it would be useful to adopt a think-tank approach in which all of you, or a number of key people, work together to develop the vision as a group. You then increase the chances of all of you holding the same vision.

It is the job of the leader to make sure that the vision stays clear, fresh and bright in people's minds, and that it is held with sufficient consistency by everyone. One of the fascinating things about organisations is that each member of it has a slightly different perspective, a different view from everyone else.

You may know the poem about the six blind men who were confronted with an elephant, and who each tried to understand what an elephant was by referring to another concept which was already familiar to him. Thus one, reaching out to touch the elephant's side, thought that an elephant must therefore be like a wall; another grasped the elephant's ear and decided it was like a fan. The third found the elephant's leg and immediately felt that the elephant must be like a tree, and so on.

So as the leader, you must constantly be testing what the people in the organisation are doing against the vision, and continuously adjusting it to keep on course. Just as the skipper of a ship is constantly referring to compass and charts, and moving the tiller to keep on course, so must the leader make adjustments and corrections all the time. I read somewhere recently that, if you don't correct your direction, you are likely to get to where you're heading!

Reiterate the vision. This means that you frequently refer to the vision, always using it to evaluate how the organisation is progressing. A vision carefully written down in a mission statement, hung on the wall and forgotten about might as well not exist. The leader must take every opportunity to refer to the vision in discussion and decisions.

Be focussed. The vision acts as a way of gathering energy towards itself. The leader should demonstrate a concentration of energy on the vision and on the tasks identified as leading towards the achievement of the vision. You should not allow distractions to interfere with the main purpose for which the organisation exists.

Remain sensitive to the environment. At the same time, it is essential that the leader keeps a close watch on trends in the environment in which the business operates. Networks and contacts with others should be carefully fostered and maintained. Trends in the economy, the political arena and social values should be closely monitored, always with a view to shaping the organisation's operations to take greatest advantage.

The leader also needs to keep abreast of things not directly related to the organisation. Lack of balance in your private life results in a skewed perspective on the organisation, and fatal tunnel vision can set in. You need to have a broad range of interests, many friends in different fields and a lively interest in the world at large. A well developed sense of community service doesn't go astray either.

Spend time on your top priorities. The clearest message you can send to other people is how you spend your time at work. If you are on about excellent service, then you should be spending at least 50% of your day at work clearly and visibly on things which will improve service. This could be as simple as giving a compliment to someone whom you caught providing exceptional service, or as major as arranging a massive training effort to enhance service. But whatever it is, it must be dedicated to your vision.

The rest of the organisation will pay lip service, if that, to a vision which is hanging on the wall but on which the boss spends no time.

The other members will take notice if the leader shows personal focus and dedication to the vision. The only way in which this can be demonstrated in a daily sense is by the clear apportionment of a major part of each day to the activity.

Never miss a chance on the soapbox. Every chance you get to talk to staff, to your boss or to outsiders should be seized and used to reinforce the vision. A few short sentences will do. It's not a bad idea to have a short speech in your head, with many variations so that people hear the same message, phrased differently each time. A visit to the plant, the office and the delivery bay can each be used to give a version of the speech. Whether the audience is one person or a thousand, the presence of the leader communicating the vision helps to keep the minds of the workers firmly on it.

Care for the staff. They are the only resource you have to bring the vision to reality. It doesn't matter how carefully you plan, how much money you invest or how clever your marketing campaign is, if the people in your organisation are not with you, hearts and minds. They can undermine or sabotage your best-laid plans, sometimes without malice aforethought but simply because you have not shared the vision with them correctly. A leader will always treat the staff with the respect and trust they deserve as human beings.

Recognition. It is very important that the leader should take every opportunity to notice when a staff member has performed in such a way as to further the vision or demonstrate the values of the organisation, and takes steps to applaud and recognise it. The recognition doesn't have to be material; what is really important is the emotional pay-off gained when the person is made to feel good about what he or she did. Even if a bonus or a material reward is involved, the emotional reward of compliments and being made to feel good should always be there as well.

Perhaps the ultimate form of recognition is promotion, and this is another opportunity for the leader to show his or her commitment to the vision. Promotions should visibly go to the people who represent and live the vision, and not the people who are "next in line" for a particular job.

In one organisation I worked in some very surprising promotions were made, and it would be true to say that a number of people felt very bitter at having been passed over. But the organisation was shown, as a result, that the expected advancement of those who think they are positioned for their boss' job does not happen any more. The promotions go to the unlikely people who have shown creativity and an understanding of the vision of the organisation, even if there is some risk involved in advancing those outside runners.

Innovation. The lifeblood of any organisation is a continuous flow of new ideas and new ways of doing things. You, as the leader, must foster innovation, and this means tolerating failures and mistakes. The self-esteem of the organisation needs to be developed so that it is able to take risks with confidence and make, if necessary, extraordinary efforts to achieve success despite the risk. At all levels of the organisation, people must feel able to contribute their ideas on how the work could be done better, and given enough space to bring it to fruition.

Pride. Every organisation has a ready-made team of ambassadors who can shape its reputation in the business community and the world in general. I refer of course to the workforce of the organisation. Every time one of your employees is asked in a social or business situation to describe his or her work, there is an opportunity to promote the organisation. In order to do this well, the employee must be proud to be employed by that organisation, and must speak about his or her work with enthusiasm. This pride must be a part of the leader's vision, and must be fostered at every opportunity.

Being a leader is demanding. It needs dedication and constant fine tuning. The leader must be sufficiently secure in his or her self to review each incident and work out what to do better next time. But the rewards are a committed workforce, an organisation with meaning and purpose and a tremendous sense of achievement, not just for the top executives but for everyone in the organisation. Corporate winners need to work on being leaders.

FURTHER READING ON LEADING AND MOTIVATING

ANSETT, Bob, *Bob Ansett, An Autobiography*, John Kerr Pty Ltd, Melbourne, 1986.

BERTRAND, John, *Born to Win*, Bantam Books, New York, 1985.

BLANCHARD, Kenneth, and JOHNSON, Spencer, *The One Minute Manager*, Willow Books, London, 1983.

IACOCCA, Lee, *Iacocca, An Autobiography*, Bantam Books, New York, 1984.

PETERS, Tom, *Thriving on Chaos: Handbook for a Management Revolution*, Macmillan, London, 1987

PETERS, Tom, and AUSTIN, Nancy, *A Passion For Excellence*, Collins, London, 1985.

ROGERS, Buck, *Getting the Best ... Out of Yourself and Others*, Harper and Row, New York, 1987.

TICHY, Noel M., and DEVANNA, Mary Anne, *The Transformational Leader*, John Wiley and Sons Inc., 1986.

WATERMAN, Robert H., *The Renewal Factor*, Bantam Books, New York, 1987.

WOODWARD, Harry, and BUCHHOLZ, Steve, *AFTERSHOCK: Helping People Through Corporate Change*, John Wiley & Sons, Inc., New York, 1987.

10

The Way That You Say It

In one of my former organisations, a government-run utility, the tradition until recently was that engineers ran everything and the most important value was engineering excellence of production.

Many of the workers in the organisation quite liked it that way. They could use the military as a model for correct behaviour and chains of command. Most things were pretty predictable because the engineers who were the managers had a preference for conservatism and straight line thinking. So, provided you did your job as well as you could and didn't create any problems, you could go home each night to get on with whatever you did in your leisure time.

However the funds made available by the government for the service provided by this organisation began to reduce in real terms over the years, and top management felt very hard pressed to spread the available funds over the demands for service. It became necessary to think through the standards which were applied to the product and the way in which the work was carried out.

With the arrival of a new chief executive who, much to everyone's dismay, was not himself an engineer, the organisation found new demands for accountability placed on it. And just to add to the discomfort of the managers, the new leader was passionate about the need to manage people better.

By this he meant, specifically, better communication and more sharing of information, better consultation at all levels, and a concerted effort towards performance appraisal, training and development. Furthermore, managers were expected to take these responsibilities upon themselves and were not allowed to pass them on to the personnel specialists. He also revitalised the the Human Resources Division and gave it top executive status in the organisation, to reflect the importance placed on the function by the new CEO. Managers who were perceived as not carrying out their responsibility for the people working for them were quickly helped to decide to work somewhere else.

Most of the recent books on management now emphasise the people issues. They are unanimous in insisting on greater involvement in decision making, and especially in drawing ideas for improvements and new ways of doing work from the people actually doing it.

What this requires is a new concept of the role people play in any organisation. There was a time when the management of "men" was considered simply as a part of the means of production, a resource to be managed along with money, materials and machines. Unfortunately many managers still think along these lines. Modern thinking, however, recognises that people provide enormous leverage if managed well, and can make the difference between OK performance and excellent performance.

Part of the difficulty many managers have stems from the inescapable fact that people are unpredictable. Many managers, and dare I say especially engineers, have risen to their current positions because of a successful track record in managing predictable resources, or at least predictable in comparison with the human being.

Many organisations have a major weakness in my opinion, which admittedly, especially in the government sector, they are generally trying hard to overcome and are slowly succeeding. The weakness is a reluctance to handle ambiguity, and a decided preference for the concrete, the known, the tangible. When dealing with the imponderables of people management, the tendency is to hide heads under blankets and hope that whatever the problem is will resolve itself.

COMMUNICATING

How often does something which absolutely and positively should never have gone wrong do just that because of a breakdown in communication? And how often could the disaster have been avoided if A had simply informed B that there was a potential problem? And if A did inform B, did B understand fully what the problem was and what its possible results were likely to be?

Probably the most difficult matter to get right in any organisation is this need for proper communication. It doesn't seem to matter whether the organisation is large or small, managed well or badly, decentralised or concentrated in one location, diversified or specialised, there are still a hundred instances a day of lack of effective communication.

One of the problems seems to arise when there is, in fact, no progress made on a particular issue to be communicated. Managers who are very meticulous about communicating action or results seem not to be conscious of the effects of their silence when nothing has occurred. The employees are often acutely aware that nothing is being communicated, and tend to feel that the reason for the silence is that things are going on behind their backs that the top executives are keeping to themselves. I don't know what they think the executives do with their time! Nevertheless the feeling is real and if not checked will grow like a fungus on the fragile plant of trust which a good manager is coaxing along. Regular reporting to your staff, even when there is nothing to report, can keep this problem at a manageable level.

Another difficulty is related to just who is doing the communicating. Jeanette Enright of Telecom Australia has done some original thinking on this vexed topic. She believes that there are only three people in any organisation from whom communication is regarded as authentic, and whose communication therefore is noted and accepted as such. The three are first, the chief executive, who not only runs the organisation but is heard in the media and seen in public forums. The second is the local version of the chief executive, perhaps a department head or a regional manager. The third is a person's own immediate supervisor. Jeanette believes that communication to staff from any other source is perceived by the staff themselves to be unreliable, irrelevant and negligible.

One of the leading consultants in the area of corporate communication, T.J. Larkin, goes even further. He says that the only effective communication is about the values of the employees, and not the values of the senior managers or the business strategists. So, if you try to communicate about quality, for example, which is a management value, you will simply not get through. Furthermore, Larkin says that the only way to communicate with employees is by personal appearance - you can forget all the glossy annual reports, and the only person they want to have communication with is their own immediate supervisor.

The most frustrating thing that can happen to a manager is when he or she has gone to elaborate lengths to communicate and then hears a few days later that "there has been no communication about this". I have a view that communication offered by a manager is not always recognised as such by the recipients. Possibly the manager is not being clear enough that the information being given is, in fact, under the heading of communication. My experience is that, in order for communication to be recognised as such, you need to metaphorically wrap up your communication in gift paper, tie it up with a big bow, and present it with some fanfare, "Hey, gang, come over here, I've got something to communicate to you".

I once came across an office situation where the general manager had sent out a memo to all staff saying, without any details, that there would have to be a rearrangement of office allocations to accommodate some new recruits. About four weeks later, the staff were most unhappy to find that, with only a few minutes notice or none at all, their office walls were being pulled down. The general manager was quite hurt when someone told him that people were upset - as far as he was concerned he had communicated what was going to happen and individuals should have known what to expect.

Communication must be two-way, and feedback is essential to the communication process. A manager who simply informs people about something that is happening is not communicating, only sending out a message. Without seeking the thoughts and reactions of the recipients of the message to its content, the manager is unable to test for correct interpretation of the content. How often have you encountered a situation where, although you thought you quite clearly stated that something was to be done, your message was interpreted as saying that it was not to be done?

The only means you have of ensuring that the true message has been received is through feedback.

Many managers feel uncomfortable asking for feedback. They think that imparting the information should suffice and that the subsequent discussion necessary to test for correct reception and reinforce the communication is an unnecessary waste of their time. A manager with this view will never be able to manage people correctly, and it is doubtful whether he or she is competent in the current job held, let alone fitted for advancement.

The method of communication also changes its effectiveness. Whether written, electronic or personal media are used depends to some extent on the circumstances. In a centralised, small organisation, face to face communication is quite likely to be used as the preferred approach, while larger organisations tend to rely more on the written word. In my opinion every organisation should adopt the face to face means as the primary way of communicating. If size or spread make it impracticable for the originator of the message to be present in person, then the local manager and local supervisors should be responsible for the communication.

For example, in an organisation I know very well, all new personnel management policies are agreed to by a corporate management group comprising all the directors of the organisation. But having been approved, it becomes the responsibility of the directors to introduce the policy into their own divisions. The staff of the Human Resources Division are there to assist, advise on implementation and generally help it to come to fruition, but the ownership of the initiative is taken squarely by line managers. This enables staff at all levels in the organisation to be informed of the new policies, taught how to use them and put them into practice, and they are able to discuss them at local level and implement them in the most appropriate way for their circumstances. This cascade approach to the transmission of information is very effective.

WAYS OF COMMUNICATING

How communication occurs will depend on the technological resources available to the organisation, but many of the basic communication means are now common in businesses. They are described in order of impact - from most effective to least effective.

Personal. The most difficult thing for many people to do - ie appear personally and talk to individuals or groups about things that affect them or in which they have an interest, just happens to be the single most effective form of communication there is.

It really means something when someone can say "I was talking to the boss the other day and she said...". The staff member gets a feeling of being in contact with the people who make the decisions and therefore feels involved and good about it.

Nothing - but nothing - beats the personal touch.

Informal appearances by the communicator are probably the best, most effective way to both get a message across and ensure it is correctly received and interpreted. In this situation both parties have the opportunity to ask questions, contribute to the development of the idea and to agree on the best way to take the required action. For effectiveness it is the tops, provided of course that it is done with frankness and sincerity. The disadvantage is the time it requires for the communicator to go and speak to everyone individually.

Telephone. The telephone provides a slightly quicker means of individual communication, especially where distances are involved. It is such a commonplace item in our daily lives as well as in business that a telephone call is almost as good as a personal visit. It has the additional advantage of a certain degree of privacy, and it enables concealment of many of the non-verbals, and thus it is slightly easier for some people to feel confident in speaking on the phone. However that same advantage has the corresponding downside - the person on the other end may feel you are hiding something, simply because you are invisible and he or she cannot check your non-verbal signals for consistency with your words.

Intercom. There are now some variations of the telephone technology which enable personal communication to occur. One of these is the intercom, which is increasing in use especially in large organisations where there are many people who need quick access to each other. It is not private - in fact talking on the intercom to the boss in a loud voice is a status symbol in many organisations, and it tends to be available only to a select few senior people. It is usually quicker than the phone but less intimate.

Telecommunications. Another possibility is the use of tele-conferencing, which makes it possible for a number of people to hook up their phones so they can have a meeting without being present. This can be useful when it is necessary to get the same message correctly understood by a group of people who are scattered geographically. It is only really effective when the voices of all the parties are distinctive or well known to each other, as trying to work out just who is speaking interferes with the reception and understanding of the information being thus transmitted.

Video. More and more organisations are using video as a means of making personal communication in such a way that everyone receives the same message. This technology is becoming cheaper and more readily available, and it is proving to be quite effective in sending messages. However by definition it is one way communication.

I have found video to be most effective when it is used as a discussion starter in small work groups, led by the group's supervisor. The supervisor introduces the video, plays it and then the group can discuss the matters contained in it. If there are any questions which the supervisor can't handle, the supervisor can undertake to get an answer and pass it on to the group later.

Feedback on the video should be collected by the supervisor from the group's comments and passed on to the source of the communication.

In the pilot's dispute of 1989, new ways of communicating were given a real boost, as people could not easily move themselves around the country to achieve face to face communication. It remains to be seen if people will return to their former level of travelling for business purposes after having tried some of the alternative technologies that are now available and improving all the time.

Very exciting possibilities for communicating, especially for training purposes, are being developed using interactive videodisc technology. A laser disc just like the compact discs from which you get such fine sound quality for your favourite music is used to record visuals and sound which are capable of instant access. Thus it is possible to see a video, listen to explanations at one or several levels of technical difficulty, go back to ensure understanding and pass an examination on the subject matter, all at the student's own learning pace. This is the training technology of the near future, and also has enormous possibilities for sales promotions and corporate communications.

Meetings and conferences. Meetings are often given special attention in the books and articles about time management, and are treated as perhaps the biggest time wasters of all. And so they are if they are regarded mechanistically, as having no other purpose than the ostensible reason for the meeting. But meetings accomplish a great deal more than their stated purpose (indeed, as the books point out, very often they don't even accomplish that!). They do provide opportunities for alliances to form, trust to be built, knowledge and understanding of the other people in the meeting, which helps to build up relationships and shared experiences. Most importantly, provided they are properly chaired, they help to make better decisions for the organisation, because the diversity of different points of view are brought to bear on each issue, thus avoiding a narrow approach.

Speeches. The last major form of personal communication is at formal presentations and speeches. This is a great way of making points which a large number of people need to hear, often gets published in written form as well so you get the advantage of being able to refer to it later, and allows the audience to get a firsthand impression of the speaker. The disadvantage is that so many people are not confident of their abilities to speak in public, and allow lack of preparation and lack of technique to feed their fear and their negative self-perceptions, so their presentation fails to achieve its intended impact.

The traditional means of communicating is by written materials : memos, letters and reports. This style of communication is impersonal and often has the result of making the documents more important than the issue being considered. How often have you expressed frustration at the behaviour of officials in government departments who go by the book and can't see that your particular set of circumstances requires a flexible interpretation of the rules, and not blind adherence to rigid procedures?

Whilst written communications have the great advantage of permanence, they are best used for transmitting factual information or material which is not intended to change the attitudes of the receivers. Manuals of procedures, for example, are found in many bureaucracies (and I include most large organisations in that term, not just government bodies) and enable a degree of equity to be applied to situations being handled by a large number of people in different places.

Less formal written communications, such as newsletters, bulletins and posters, tend to have more impact, probably because their style is more likely to involve some of the very people at whom it is aimed. They get wide readership and are often taken home to show the family.

Some organisations publish a regular document listing internal job vacancies, announcing promotions etc, but also containing items about personal health, clubs which are being formed, career opportunities and other items of general interest to staff.

As Director - Human Resources in an organisation which published weekly "Personnel Notices", I wrote a regular "100 Words" column, in which I would take a single issue, whatever had come to my notice during the week as needing some attention or clarification, and saying very simply the message I wished to convey. I took it as a challenge to make my point in exactly one hundred words, neither more nor less, and this had the engineers counting for the first few appearances. But the feedback I got told me that it was well received as a light-handed way of getting a point across without being directive. It cost me some effort to crank this out every week without fail, but the results were worth it.

Probably the fastest-growing and most exciting development in this area is electronic communications of various sorts. Electronic mail and office automation allow messages to be sent to one person or to hundreds, simultaneously. It can be very personal or completely formal. The messages can be filed either electronically or printed out and retained as hard copy.

The importance of frequent, personal and effective communication, in upwards, downwards and sideways directions cannot be over-emphasised for a good manager of people. He or she must be able to use different media to suit different purposes and to get the advantages of each medium whilst minimising the disadvantages, perhaps by using a mix of media so that they balance and reinforce each other.

Allen E. Murray, Chairman and President of the Mobil Corporation, USA, tells how his company went overboard, or so the top executives thought, in improving communications with its employees. Meetings, videos, newsletters, bulletins and everything else they could think of were pouring through the company. Then a survey of staff was conducted, and what do you think was the major concern about the organisation which showed up in the results? Lack of communication! Not enough effort was being placed on the personal, by the immediate supervisors and managers.

The open door policy is now almost a laughable cliche, but it still has value. The door is open for you, manager or supervisor or managing director, to go out of. Only by moving among your people, and constantly being in touch with what they are doing and what their concerns are, will you be able to frame your communications to address their real concerns and not what you imagine to be their interest s and concerns. There is no point in communicating the things which are of little interest, if you do not first address the things which are.

FURTHER READING ON THE ART OF COMMUNICATING

ELGIN, Suzette Haden, *The Last Word on the Gentle Art of Verbal Self-Defense,* Prentice Hall Press, New York, 1987.

LARKIN, T. J., *Communicating With Employees: What Works, What Doesn't,* Institute of Personnel Management of Australia, Melbourne, 1989.

11

Change, Development And Growth

A very senior executive, Bob, telephoned me to talk about a member of his staff who had applied for a promotion to a different area and was not going to be successful because of certain inconsistencies of behaviour on the job. I had on a previous occasion encouraged Bob to have a frank and open talk with his subordinate, using appropriate language and non-verbals. As a manager, Bob was one of the best in the organisation at communicating, being open to new ideas, knowing his staff and all the rest. He was ringing now to report on his recent discussion with his staff member. He was also quite hurt and upset.

"And I'm really staggered," he told me, "because the guy is desperately keen to get a promotion, but he's on the engineers' training scheme and doesn't want to give that up, and he's really enjoying what he's learning in his present job. We talked about his performance and he said he'd have liked to talk to someone about things, so I asked him why he hadn't come to me before to talk. And he told me - I'm still not approachable! It's been a lesson for me - and it's hurting, right now, but I'm making an action plan to get out and about more."

Bob had stumbled across a classic example of the single most common reason why things go wrong in organisations: lack of feedback.

GIVING FEEDBACK

Probably nobody ever gives you any feedback about your performance at work. This is even more likely to be the case if you are actually doing quite well and nothing is going wrong. But very often someone is performing well below either capacity or expectations, and nobody ever tells them. Indeed, workmates will often cover up for a poor performer, out of a mistaken sense of pity or protectiveness, and never tackle the issue head on. If you have ever had to deal with an employee who was an alcoholic or drug addict, you will know what I mean.

As a career development consultant I am constantly confronted with situations where someone has applied for a promotion and, being unsuccessful, took advantage of an opportunity to ask why. They are often horrified to discover that they are regarded as inferior performers, and the most frequent response is "Why didn't somebody tell me before?"

It is very tempting for a manager to shy away from giving someone unpleasant news. But the manager who does not face up to this very basic part of dealing with people is simply sparing himself or herself the emotional hardship of speaking out, and is being grossly unfair to the subordinate concerned. It is a demonstration of selfishness and raises grave doubts about the manager's fitness for further advancement if he or she will not do the right thing by helping people to develop and grow.

That is not to say that blunt negative remarks or outspoken criticism is needed. The manager must be sufficiently well acquainted with the individual to couch the terms of any feedback in such a way that it will get the message over clearly and still preserve the person's self esteem.

Giving feedback. The focus should be on the behaviour, rather than on the individual's personal characteristics. This approach makes it much easier on the manager, who usually has to psych himself or herself up to the task. If you pick out the facts of the occurrence, and discuss frankly with your subordinate what actually happened, you can then both use the objectivity of the facts to balance your natural emotional reactions.

The same applies to feedback in the form of praise. The real value of feedback is to enable you both to work out what was good and should be practised more often, and what could be improved next time. Unspecific praise, eg "That was very good" is gratifying to your subordinate, but it is not very helpful in working out what was good about it. It would be much more useful to say "I like the way you kept cool while that customer was having a go at the product", and such a remark reinforces the good behaviour for the next occasion.

Feedback can and should be offered to your peers and your superiors in the organisation too. Everyone loves a compliment, and perhaps the more senior the other person is, the more your feedback should be couched in positive terms. However, if there is something that you really feel needs attention or could be handled better, there are several ways to approach the topic with delicacy and in a climate of trust.

I often have to say something like this to a manager in a client organisation: "I think we have a problem in the matter of... It seems that your statement to the meeting on Wednesday was misinterpreted by the group, and they feel that you are out to reduce the workforce by the introduction of this technology. They don't seem to have picked up your other comments about the three-year time frame for the reduction. What can we do to correct this impression?"

The technique is simple. First, I have indicated that it is a shared problem, not the manager's problem alone, by using "we". Second, I haven't said that he made a very forceful statement that staff numbers were expected to reduce by 50% as a result of the new equipment, which had the effect of focussing everyone's attention on that and not on the rest of the message. Instead I have phrased it to draw attention to the impression created, rather than his misdirected communication. And thirdly, I have given him recognition for what he actually meant to convey and asked him for ideas on how to re-emphasise it. Instead of getting upset with me, this executive will appreciate my concern that his true message is correctly received and will turn his attention on how to correct the wrongly received signals.

Oddly enough, although most people enjoy giving compliments, they don't do it very often. Some managers fear that by complimenting or praising a subordinate too often, they will develop an inflated opinion of themselves and start to threaten the manager's superiority. Others take the view that people are paid to come to work and do their jobs in an appropriate manner, and therefore that someone who does well is simply doing what is required. These managers miss many wonderful opportunities to make their people feel good about themselves, so that they stretch further and do even better. Surely continual improvement is what we are striving for, and it simply cannot be achieved without constant and relevant feedback.

Seeking feedback is another very important part of being a good manager of people. Just like anyone else, you are dependent upon feedback to find out how you are performing. You should be seeking feedback actively, every day, from everyone in your working environment - your boss, your peers, your staff and your customers. If you don't, you run a terrible risk - the risk of coasting along and never fine-tuning your direction.

I read somewhere recently that the manager has to be like the skipper of a boat, setting a course for a particular destination. But the vessel doesn't always point directly to the destination and simply go there: there are all sorts of obstacles and channels to avoid or to follow, and so the navigator has to steer the course constantly correcting the bearings but always heading generally in the direction of the goal. The message to managers is: if you don't continuously monitor your direction and correct your course, you're likely to get to where you're heading!

So you need feedback too, perhaps even more than you need to give feedback to your people.

It takes guts.

It takes strength of character to listen to someone telling you that something is wrong, and even more to refrain from defending your actions or your position and set about correcting the problem. But that is the only way you will be able to manage your tasks effectively.

Information is the lifeblood of any organisation, and you need as much as you can get, whether it is palatable or not. When you get it, act on it. If you are in doubt as to its validity, test it by all means, but give it the benefit of the doubt. Feedback is likely to be valid as it represents someone's perceptions of the way things are, not necessarily the reality. You may need to change their perceptions rather than change the reality. But a person's perceptions are no less real for being perceptions; in many cases they are more powerful than the reality, and you need to be able to work in the area of the perceived.

Follow through. This is where you do your testing that the correct messages have been received and understood, and take any corrective action required.

There was an incident in an organisation where I worked where Gary, an inexperienced union representative, called a rather emotional stop-work meeting without going through the normal channels which require informing the union "bureaucrats" first. Gary's superiors in the union movement were rather embarrassed at the incident. The managers of the organisation took care to keep from scoring points over the issue, because they wanted to continue their hitherto open and trusting relationship with the union. However they also wanted to make sure that the breach of discipline was understood for what it was and prevent it from recurring.

The same day that the incident occurred I talked privately with Bill, the Vice President of the union, expressing my concern that this person had damaged the effectiveness of the union as a player by his impetuous action. Bill admitted to me off the record that the union was very unhappy that the incident had occurred and was greatly embarrassed by it. We then went on to discuss how Gary could be helped - by attending a training course; by having someone senior and experienced from the union help him by explaining what he did and its possible consequences, etc. I made arrangements with Bill that the matter would have to be raised in a suitable forum, and he agreed that this should be done.

It so happened that the same day there was a scheduled meeting with representatives of all the major unions in the organisation, who meet monthly with the management to discuss issues of organisational change. I was in the chair for this meeting, and raised the matter in the context of concern for the credibility of all of us and distributed the correct grievance handling procedure as set down in the award.

The loop was thus closed: the incident was allowed to drop but needed action to follow through with the person who made the error was taken, and a lesson was learnt. And the effective relationship between the management and the union was strengthened, not damaged.

Follow through means closure on whatever the situation is. It is terribly damaging to your people to leave them without any means of knowing your reactions to an incident or situation which they have created.

MANAGING PERFORMANCE

Performance management is the single major way in which your people can receive the information they need and take action to develop and improve themselves. It means formal performance appraisals at least once a year, and it also means using critical incidents as opportunities to review performance and discuss ways of improvement.

Talking frankly and helpfully to staff about their performance is probably the most difficult thing a manager has to do.

Because the manager often fears that he or she will upset the other person, the tendency is to hide behind the good things and not discuss the negatives, or only in a token fashion. If the organisation has a formal appraisal system in place, it is very tempting to simply tick the boxes and tell the person they are doing well. But in sparing himself or herself the mental stress of talking openly about performance, the manager is depriving staff of the means to grow - and in my opinion that is immoral.

It is akin to starving a baby.

You should always take care that the annual formal appraisal does not become the only time when you discuss performance is discussed with your people. There are lots of opportunities, all the time, which enable a manager to introduce the subject and offer praise, constructive criticism or positive action for improvement. Such opportunities include salary increment or bonus time, when someone applies for a promotion within the organisation, when someone has failed to obtain a promotion within the organisation and when an incident occurs on the job which the manager thinks could have been handled better.

Remember that the closer to a particular incident or event which gives the opportunity to discuss performance, the more easily you can focus on the specific behaviours demonstrated at that time, and therefore the more objective and less emotional your performance discussion will be.

Formal performance appraisal should be a two-way process between you and your associate. If your organisation has a prepared appraisal form, you should use that as the basis, but feel free to include additional items if they are important and not covered in the form. Appraisal is not a mechanistic process of filling out the form; it is an opportunity for the two of you to review how things are going and set up an action plan for the next period.

For instance, suppose I am about to hold a performance discussion with Sue, my second-in-command. I believe that any form used (and they are very helpful in structuring the discussion) should relate to the requirements of Sue's particular job, and not be a list of desired traits (punctuality, dress, politeness to the boss, etc). I use a form with a lot of blank lines, which enables me to look at Sue's position description, then fill in the major duties, personal characteristics, knowledge and skills required, and performance standards. I then evaluate her performance against those items.

While I am doing this, Sue also fills out the same form in the same way. Usually we get together first and agree on which duties, skills etc should be included in the appraisal.

Having each filled out the form and come to our individual views about performance in that job by that person, we meet - I schedule two hours to get a really open discussion going which need not be pressurised or cut short. Sue leads the discussion. She takes me through each item on the form, shows me how her self-rating went and we compare it with mine. If there is any significant difference, we talk about the reasons why. We discuss, against each item, what needs to be done to correct any shortfall in Sue's expected performance and any specific actions to make even more improvements to items well performed.

Finally we talk about Sue's career goals and needs for personal development, and make an action plan. We list training required, experience needed, knowledge and skills needed. Sometimes we list a visit to a customer or a supplier, or possibly a secondment to work for a period of time with a related organisation. The action plan always says what is required, who is to do it and a target date by when it is to be done. Then we agree on the date of the next performance appraisal, we both sign the form and we both generally feel pretty positive about the whole matter.

One of the real advantages of this approach is that, very often, the staff member being appraised rates himself or herself more harshly than I have - people are usually their own severest critics. Then I have the pleasure of giving praise and encouragement, and help to build up the other person's self-confidence.

The hardest part is for you to psych yourself up to doing the right thing by your people. You might feel it's impertinent to talk to others about themselves, or simply shrink from a task you think is going to be unpleasant or cause someone distress. In fact performance appraisal is the greatest act of kindness you could ever do for your people - giving them real information about how they are regarded and helping them to grow both personally and within the organisation.

TRAINING AND DEVELOPMENT

Training is probably the single thing which will help organisations survive into the next century. Organisations are gearing themselves up to spending anywhere between 1% and 10% of the total payroll on training. (Under the new Commonwealth Government policy, organisations are expected to invest 1% to 1.5% of employee costs in training.) At least one training opportunity per year for each employee is becoming normal expectation.

You only have to look at the way technology is changing how work is done to see that a whole range of new knowledge and skills are needed in the workforce. All of a sudden, even professionally trained people are desperately keen to learn touch-typing!

Even more importantly, people need help to change the old ways and give them up in favour of the new. And because many systems are specially developed or tailored to meet the particular requirements of the business, you can't expect to send someone to a packaged course. The training must be provided in-house, either on- or off-the-job, and must relate to the specific task.

More significant still is the rapidly growing need for management training. Managers have to learn to stop being professionals at whatever they were first qualified in, and start to learn to manage people. This is one area where you never stop learning. The latest thinking of management writers brings an exciting new dimension to the way managers can achieve their goals and bring their people along.

The fact is that the best training for work is obtained in the workplace, not in institutes of learning.

If your organisation has a training professional or a personnel manager, the first thing would be to invite that person to lunch and have a good long talk. The more you can inform the training people about your work and your business, the better they will be able to suggest training to meet your needs and those of your staff.

If there is nobody in charge of training as such, or if you are not satisfied with the service you get from the internal people, there are hundreds of training opportunities available from consultants and various organisations. The Australian Institute of Management has a college offering short courses in a range of subjects relevant to supervisors and managers. So does the Council of Adult Education, rather more broadly based to include more basic skills. The various local technical and TAFE colleges often have courses available to the public, and this can be very relevant to managers in country locations. There are also many training seminars by world experts available on cassette so you can turn travelling time into training time if your car has a player, or using a portable machine with headphones if you are a public transport commuter.

Training is not an optional extra for a manager who wants to demonstrate his or her fitness for advancement. Training is an essential part of performance management. A manager is only as good as the people who work for him or her; it is in your own very best interests to make sure they are skilled up as high as they can go and have the opportunity to develop further. Your aim should be to have them so good they are continually sought after for promotion!

While that may cause you some disruption because you then have to train somebody else, it says something about you as a manger of people. A good manager has high turnover in his or her department. (So does a bad manager, but for different reasons!)

INNOVATION

Encouraging ideas. Another mark of the good manager is if lots of ideas and improvements to the way work is carried out in the department keep bubbling up from the staff.

Too often I am talking to someone and she says something like, "I know how we could do that much quicker and people wouldn't have to wait so long for their deliveries, but when I spoke up they just laughed."

The fact is that you are much less likely to know what is wrong with your systems, or how they could be improved, than the people doing the work.

Lots of managers seem to think that having the ideas is their job, and their staff are there to carry them out. This stems from irrational fear on the manager's part that if anyone else has ideas it threatens their authority.

The result is stultifying to the staff and deprives the customer of better service. This of course makes the manger look really good in the eyes of his or her superiors!

There is a saying, "If it ain't broke, don't fix it". That's OK for motor cars maybe, but in business the manager should be constantly on the lookout for things which will improve service to the customers and the efficiency of staff, even if the existing arrangements are working satisfactorily.

You will find it takes a little time to get people freed up so they are comfortable making suggestions. There are lots of devices that can be used - suggestion boxes, innovation awards, incentives etc., but the whole thing will be pretty hollow if you are not going to adopt more than a few of the suggestions. People need to see their ideas being taken up and used in order to get a feeling of trust that you really mean what you say. The only way is to constantly reiterate the message that ideas are welcome when you talk to people, and to follow through by at least trying out every idea.

If you are confronted with an idea that is for some real reason not workable, you should ask the suggester to keep working on it, perhaps with the help of someone else, to see if the obstacle can be overcome. The very worst thing you can do is to reject an idea out of hand; any rejected ideas should entitle the suggester to an explanation of the reasons for the rejection.

DELEGATION

Delegation is a term which is widely misunderstood. Some managers seem to think it is a way that they can get out of work, others think it is an abrogation of their jobs. In fact it is the only means a manager has of obtaining leverage on his or her time.

A manager is paid, not for time and labour, but for judgment and influence. It follows that a manager's work output is not in work done by the manager personally, but in the work done by the people under that manager's control. The manager is responsible for the total outputs of his or her department. As such the manager should be spending management time on the judgment and influence part of the job, and not on the actual work.

Lack of delegation is a classic reason why managers are pressed for time. They think that in order to get a thing done right, they have to do it themselves, or at least keep close supervision over the doing. They are so busy doing things that they run out of time to get things done!

Lack of proper delegation cheats your staff of opportunities to develop and learn new things. If you maintain a jealous watch on a process, your employee is unable to learn by feel and will constantly be referring (and deferring) to you, so the job gets done by rote. The employee will not be any more skilled and confident the next time he or she is asked to do that same task, because you have interfered with the learning process with your close surveillance. You are using the other person as the physical instrument of the task, just like a machine, and you have retained the mental aspects of the task. This close guardianship of the mental aspects often results from a reluctance, deep down, to share knowledge in case it threatens the manager's position.

Proper delegation is very simple. You first need to sit down and work out exactly what you want the other person to do, expressed in terms of the output, i.e. the final result. Then you need to decide how much discretion you should allow the other person to do the task. An experienced person with good knowledge of the organisation could probably be left completely alone to work out how the task is to be done and to obtain whatever resources are needed for its completion. A less experienced or less confident person will need help from you at the time the task is delegated, so you could talk through how the task should be done and what resources might be needed.

Any fixed constraints should be decided between you at the outset, and a time agreed for the completion of the task.

Then leave the person alone to get on with it.

If you detect that there are problems before the task is completed, you should ask the person some not too threatening questions. Are there any difficulties preventing the task being done? Are any additional resources needed? Is anyone being unhelpful? Does the person need you to clear any roadblocks? If you have a good trusting relationship with your staff member, he or she will feel pleased that you are taking an interest and will ask for any needed help, without feeling inadequate or crowded by you.

When the task is done, praise the effort which the person put in and the parts which were done well. If anything is not done correctly, don't criticise, but explain what is wrong and discuss ways to get it right. On no account take the task back yourself or give it to someone else to fix up! It's the fastest way to alienate everybody.

TEACHING AND COACHING

Managers have to learn to let their people try, fail and make mistakes. If no mistakes are being made nobody is learning and growing.

Instructing. An important part of the manager's job is the role of teacher. Much of what has already been covered in this chapter amounts to teaching: giving feedback, discussing performance, and delegating correctly. But there are techniques of instruction on the job which when used make the learning tasks of a new employee or an experience employee learning new skills or procedures much more efficient.

As a manager, you should carefully analyse the task and decide on the main steps to be achieved. These are the milestones along the way. Each of these main steps almost certainly has a number of key points which need to be observed - where to get a needed resource, what you need to have handy before starting each main step, etc. The task should be thought of as a recipe and written out just like that. Then you can demonstrate the task one or several times, explaining each main step and key point as the demonstration goes along.

Then the lesson plan should provide for the learner to practice, at first under your supervision, so you can make sure all the main steps and key points are observed, and when a bit of skill and confidence is developed, alone. You should return from time to time to make sure that the procedure is being done correctly and to help sort out any difficulties.

Finally you should give the learner feedback on the performance of the new task and congratulate his or her achievement of learning a new skill.

The process requires the investment of some time by the manager in thinking through the task and breaking it down into the main steps and key points, but it is time very well spent. Remember, if the person doesn't learn the task correctly, it's the manager's fault.

WHAT ALL THIS MEANS FOR A MANAGER

This chapter has placed great emphasis on the need for the manager to accept the development of people as his or her primary responsibility. It means developing your people so that they know more than you do, become better than you are and leave you because they get promoted. This philosophy can cause problems for middle managers especially, because they have built up their power base upon having access to knowledge and a degree of expertise. They feel that if they share their knowledge they will lose power, if they talk to their people they will show weakness, that if they train people up they will show up badly themselves, if they seek ideas from others they are losing face, that if they delegate they will lose control.

The fact is that management is about people, and people represent the success of the organisation. A manager who is so concerned with preserving his or her own power base that he or she is afraid to develop the staff is cheating the customers, the shareholders, the boss and the staff of the best the organisation can offer.

I have constantly found that the more I communicate, the more power I share and give to others, the more influential and respected I become.

FURTHER READING ON DEVELOPING PEOPLE

BLANCHARD, Kenneth, and LORBER, Robert, *Putting the One Minute Manager to Work*, William Morrow and Company Inc., New York, 1984.

HEWITT-GLEESON, Michael, *Software for the Brain*, Wrightbooks, Melbourne, 1989.

HICKMAN, Craig R., and SILVA, Michael A., *Creating Excellence*, Unwin Paperbacks, London, 1985.

SMITH, Neville, and AINSWORTH, Murray, *Ideas Unlimited*, Nelson, Melbourne, 1985.

12

Building The Team

As I tried to show in the first chapter, organisations depend on relationships, upwards, downwards and sideways. More and more organisations are now being structured to emphasise the sideways relationships, either through flatter structures with fewer reporting layers, or through a matrix style where semi-autonomous groups form to accomplish a particular task, then dissolve, and the people involved re-form themselves into new teams to do something else.

Traditionally, a manager or supervisor is in a power position because of access to information. This information may not be complete, and it may have come from dubious sources, but the fact is that it is information which is not possessed by other people working for that manager. So the manager can use the information to bargain with, to dispense favours or to show disapproval. How many times have you seen situations where the manager has taken someone in to the office, closed the door and told them secrets?

This power is now being shattered by the exponential growth of information technology. Instead of being exclusive, information is now more readily available to people who would not have had access to it, but now they have a computer on every desk, or nearly. Furthermore, there is actually more information being produced than ever before. So the traditional power base of a supervisor is eroded.

There is a change in the attitudes of management to unions, too, especially in the matter of sharing information about the organisation's financial performance, threats and opportunities.

Staff now have the right to be consulted on a number of specific issues, and their expectations of being consulted and involved are growing.

All this causes a lot of trouble for the manager or supervisor who has developed his or her power base in the traditional way. Modern management is now asking these people to give up their rights to exclusive information, to share it and to allow other people to use it. It is very frightening because it is taking away the only weapon that they have, leaving them exposed in the world.

And they are finding that they are required to develop their interpersonal skills, encourage others to learn and to allow them to take risks. Leadership becomes their weapon rather than information. But they need to develop a new way of thinking about the people working for them in order to give the right kind of leadership. In particular, they have to learn to trust people.

INFORMATION FOR EVERYONE

Sharing your information is a good way to start developing that trust. By telling people all that you can about their own work performance, about the organisation's performance, about the pressures which are on the organisation and what the future might hold, how the competitors are performing, etc., you are implicitly inviting their contribution to the management of the organisation. Being entrusted with this very basic kind of information, in my experience, is wonderfully empowering for most people, and soon you will be receiving all kinds of ideas to make the business more competitive and perform better.

If you have been, hitherto, the kind of manager who thinks your authority is challenged by a subordinate who comes up with a good idea, your future in the 1990s is very limited. Businesses need all the creativity and innovation they can get in order to keep whatever frail global competitiveness our country has. By resisting or discouraging contributions for improvement from the people who know best how to improve productivity and customer service, you are allowing personal protectiveness to get in the way of your organisation's growth, not to mention your own.

Know your people - build rapport and trust, and your rewards will be remarkable. The pressures on managers this decade is to establish team goals and to measure team performance, not individual performance. Your ability to get the team working correctly is your performance criterion as a successful manager.

DEALING WITH UNIONS

Union representatives and officials are, I hope it's not really necessary to remind you, part of the team too. If you take a bit of trouble to get to know your employees' representatives personally, and use the negotiation approach described in Chapter 6, then you should be on good ground when you need to get their co-operation.

On many occasions I have been able to obtain union agreement to things which are not totally in accordance with union policy, but because of our good relationship and a general openness of communication, was accepted.

Some people will be snarling at this point that the employer is in charge and doesn't have to seek approval by union representatives to do anything. Whether this is true or not, my experience is that the path is much, much smoother if you take the time to keep the unions informed about the organisation's performance, threats and opportunities, and involve them in problem solving. The right communication with the right union representative can get you out of trouble or prevent you from getting into it, and it is not worth it to take an arrogant standpoint.

When a union representative comes to see you, schedule a generous amount of time for the discussion. Offer a cup of tea or coffee and allow some time for a general chat about the weather, the football or whatever. The rapport you establish will set the tone for the substance of your discussion.

Even better, initiate contact with the union representatives when there is no particular matter of concern, but simply to keep in touch. Don't settle for a formal once-a-month meeting; that appears to be an easy way but it is likely to become an organised grizzle session. It is far better to connect with the shop steward frequently and informally, building up a relationship of mutual respect and trust.

MANAGING YOUR BOSS

It may not have occurred to you that a good proportion of your management role is managing upwards - in other words, managing your boss and your boss' bosses. But they are part of the team, too.

It is your responsibility to create and nurture an effective working relationship with your boss, just as much as it is with your peers and subordinates. In fact, if you really want to be a corporate winner, you will do more that your boss expects you to do and more than you are paid to do. A major element of job satisfaction is to give as much as you can, regardless of whether you are directly compensated for it.

Unfortunately, many people feel that they are paid to do certain things and nothing more is required of them. This attitude disempowers you from taking control of what happens to you. It makes you a passive, powerless cog in the machine instead of a living, thinking contributor to the organisation's success and thus to your own satisfaction and prosperity.

It is in your own interest to become as valuable as possible to the organisation. The more value you give, the more valuable you become, and the more you are appreciated. It makes it easier to sell your ideas to your boss if you already have a track record of positive contribution and willingness to put effort in to make things work properly. It will give you the credibility which brings opportunities and additional responsibilities, thus increasing your control. And it is the best foundation of all for increasing your pay and other opportunities which lead to further advancement.

MANAGEMENT IN THE NEW AGE

The National Wage Case decisions which have resulted in efforts towards the restructuring of industrial awards are going to have very far-reaching effects on the way work is done and on those who are accountable for getting it done. It is not only the awards themselves which are being restructured - it is really the restructuring of work, of individual jobs. Responsibility is being placed in the redesigned jobs at the lowest level practicable in the work group - and that means that operatives will be making judgments and taking decisions which formerly had to be referred to a supervisor.

This development will be accompanied by a massive growth in industrial training. Many organisations will go well above the 1% of payroll now set by the Federal Government as the benchmark. Ordinary workers will be given training in such things as leadership, motivation, negotiation and quality control. The outcome of this, if the expectations of the government and the union movement are met, will be that ordinary workers can become more accountable for their own output and productivity, and will not need such close supervision.

All this is very good for the country, but there is a risk for supervisors and managers. With access to information technology, there will be less need for staff people whose function is mainly to act as a booster in the communications system. And with workers newly empowered to manage their own work efforts, the need for people to be employed simply to control other people will be greatly diminished.

So, I predict that supervisory and management jobs, as we currently know them, will change and reduce in numbers significantly in the next decade.

This will happen regardless of any rearguard actions on the part of the (generally non-unionised) supervisors and middle management level people. There will simply not be room on the payroll of organisations for the employment of people who neither make any decisions nor lead anybody, and whose skills are confined to the traditional ways of doing work.

There are two ways in which managers can prepare themselves for this new age of work:

First, I strongly advise you to develop your computer skills to the utmost you can. It may take some real effort, but in the next ten years nearly everyone will be a brain worker using computers, one way or another. In a list of skill requirements which was developed in the process of award restructuring for a major Australian port, computer skills were listed as one of the essential training requirements for a cleaner's position.

Another very good reason for getting familiar with computers is that your school-age children are already well advanced in the use of this technology. The people who are really using computers to their full potential right now are about 12 years old, and in less than 10 years they are going to come and work for you! Are you going to be able to manage them, leveraged with the technology as they will be, with traditional methods of discipline and control?

The other way you can prepare yourself for the next decade is to become a superb manager and leader of people. With increased knowledge and use of the techniques outlined in this book, you have the potential to play an important part in the future of your organisation. Despite all the trend to knowledge work, using brains rather than bodies to achieve outputs, people will still have their personal crises, stresses, difficulties in working alongside other, anxieties about advancement and fears for their future. These things are going to remain constant, and may get even more demanding as knowledge levels and ability to articulate increases. A manager who can handle the people side of the organisation, and can leave the process side to those who are closest to it, will be a prized commodity on the job market.

So please, don't stop here. Dip into some of the further reading recommended at the end of each chapter, and start preparing yourself for a successful and satisfying future.

FURTHER READING ON THE FUTURE FOR MANAGERS

HANDY, Charles, *The Future of Work*, Basil Blackwell Ltd., 1985.

HEGARTY, Christopher, *How To Manage Your Boss*, Ballantine Books, New York, 1984.

KRAVETZ, Dennis J., *The Human Resources Revolution*, Jossey- Bass, San Francisco, 1988.

MACCOBY, Michael, *Why Work*, Simon and Schuster, New York, 1988

MORGAN, Gareth, *Riding The Waves Of Change*, Jossey-Bass Publishers, 1988.

Bibliography

AMES, B. Charles, and HLAVACEK, James D., *Market Driven Management*, Dow Jones-Irwin, Illinois, 1989.

BATTEN, Joe D., *Tough-Minded Management*, AMACOM, New York, 1978.

BERNE, Eric, *Games People Play*, Penguin Books, 1966.

BLANCHARD, Kenneth, and JOHNSON, Spencer, *The One Minute Manager*, Willow Books, London, 1983.

BLANCHARD, Kenneth, and LORBER, Robert, *Putting the One Minute Manager to Work*, William Morrow and Company, New York, 1984.

BOTTOMLEY, Maria, *Executive Image*, Penguin Books Australia, Melbourne, 1988.

CABOT, Tracy, *How to Make a Man Fall in Love With You*, Bantam Books, Sydney, 1984.

CHAPMAN, Elwood N., *The Fifty-Minute Career Discovery Program*, Crisp Publications Inc., Los Altos, California, 1988.

CHAPMAN, Elwood N., Plan B: *Protecting Your Career From the Winds of Change*, Crisp Publications Inc., Los Altos, California, 1988.

COHEN, Herb, *You Can Negotiate Anything*, Angus and Robertson, Sydney, 1982.

DANIELS, Peter, *How To Reach Your Life Goals*, House of Tabor, 1985.

DYER, Wayne W., *Your Erroneous Zones*, Avon Books, New York, 1976.

ELGIN, Suzette Haden, *The Last Word On The Gentle Art Of Verbal Self-Defense*, Prentice Hall Press, New York, 1987.

FISHER, Roger, and URY, William, *Getting To Yes*, Hutchinson, London, 1982.

FULGHUM, Robert, *All I Really Need To Know I Learned In Kindergarten*, Grafton Books, London, 1989.

HANDY, Charles, *The Future Of Work*, Basil Blackwell, Oxford, 1985.

HARRAGAN, Betty Lehan, *Games Mother Never Taught You*, Warner Books, New York, 1977.

HARRIS, Thomas, *I'm OK - You're OK*, Pan Books Ltd, London, 1973.

HEGARTY, Christopher, *How To Manage Your Boss*, Ballantine Books, New York, 1984.

HEWITT-GLEESON, Michael, *Software For The Brain*, Wrightbooks, Melbourne, 1989.

HICKMAN, Craig, and SILVA, Michael, *Creating Excellence: Managing Corporate Culture, Strategy and Change in the New Age*, Unwin Paperbacks, London, 1986.

JEFFERS, Susan, *Feel The Fear and Do It Anyway*, Century Hutchinson Ltd., London, 1987.

JOHNSON, Kerry L., *Mastering The Game*, Louis & Ford Co., 1987.

KARP, H. B., *Personal Power*, American Management Association, New York, 1985.

KIDMAN, Antony, *From Thought to Action*, Biochemical and General Consulting Service, Sydney, 1988.

KIDMAN, Antony, *Tactics for Change*, Biochemical and General Consulting Service, Sydney, 1986.

KRAVETZ, Dennis J., *The Human Resources Revolution*, Jossey-Bass, San Francisco, 1988.

LAKEIN, Alan, *How To Get Control of Your Time and Your Life*, David McKay Co., New York, 1973.

LARKIN, T. J., *Communicating With Employees: What Works, What Doesn't*, Institute of Personnel Management of Australia, Melbourne, 1989.

LYNN, Jonathan, and JAY, Antony, *Yes Prime Minister*, BBC Publications, London, 1986.

MACCOBY, Michael, *Why Work*, Simon & Schuster, New York, 1988.

MOLLOY, John T., *Dress For Success*, Warner Books, New York, 1975.

MORGAN, Gareth, *Riding The Waves Of Change*, Jossey-Bass Publishers, 1988.

MORRIS, Desmond, *Manwatching: a Field Guide to Human Behaviour*, Triad/Panther, St. Albans, 1978.

NIERENBERG, Juliet, and ROSS, Irene, *Women and the Art of Negotiating*, Simon and Schuster Inc., New York, 1985.

ONCKEN, William, *Managing Management Time*, Prentice-Hall of Australia Pty Ltd, Sydney, 1984.

ORR, Fred, *How To Succeed At Work*, Unwin Paperbacks, Sydney, 1987.

PEASE, Alan, *Body Language: How to Read Others' Thoughts by their Gestures*, Camel Publishing Company, Sydney, 1981.

PETERS, Tom, *Thriving on Chaos: Handbook for a Management Revolution*, Macmillan, London, 1987

PETERS, Tom, and AUSTIN, Nancy, *A Passion For Excellence*, Collins, London, 1985.

ROBERTS, Jean, *Managing Time and Success*, Information Australia, Melbourne, 1987.

SMITH, Neville, and AINSWORTH, Murray, *Ideas Unlimited: the Mindmix Approach to Innovative Management*, Nelson, Melbourne, 1985.

WATERMAN, Robert H., *The Renewal Factor*, Bantam Books, New York, 1987.

WOODWARD, Harry, and BUCHHOLZ, Steve, *AFTERSHOCK: Helping People Through Corporate Change*, John Wiley & Sons, Inc., New York, 1987.

Index

action plan	23, 24, 122
advancement	8, 37, 134
aggressive behaviour	37, 38
anger	37, 38, 40, 44
anxiety	34
assertion	39
assertiveness	41
skills	67
techniques	39, 42
attitude	10, 86
Australian Institute of Management	124
behaviour	7-11, 15, 30, 37-39, 46, 57-58, 62 65, 95, 103, 111, 115-117, 121
blame	11, 15, 85
body language	37, 51, 52, 59, 62
boss	8, 9, 35, 89, 100, 134,
boss' boss	8
closed positions	60
communication	11, 103, 105-110, 112, 133
confidence	8-9, 100
conflict	67
consultation	103
control	6, 11, 15, 24, 129, 134, 135
copping out	27, 31
Council of Adult Education	124
customer service	52, 132
customers	5, 6, 10, 11, 85, 86
delegation	126
directive questions	81
dress	55-58
dumb questions	75, 78-79
electronic mail	112
eye contact	53, 54

facial expression 55
family 9
fear 8, 13-14, 16, 24, 29, 31-34, 37, 44-45, 69-70
                       86, 111, 118, 120, 125, 136
fear junkie 13
feedback 38, 89, 107, 110, 115-116, 119, 127-128
feelings 40
firmness 41
follow through 119
friendships 10
future 8, 11, 132
gestures 60-61
giving feedback 116
goals 17-18, 67, 96
guilt 45-46
honesty 40
ideas 9-10, 100, 124-125, 132, 134
industrial awards 135
influence 7-9, 11, 13, 15, 35, 38, 53-55, 58, 65, 126
initiative 30
innovation 100, 124, 132
instruction on the job 127
interactive videodisc 110
intercom 109
interests 70, 98
internal customers 86
interpersonal skills 7, 132
judgement 8, 88-89, 126
knowledge 9, 86, 89, 128
lack of communication 85
lack of delegation 126
lack of time 27-28
leadership 37, 88, 95-96, 132, 135
leading questions 81
life-work planning 16
lifeline 16
lifetime goals 17
listening 85, 87, 90
long-term 22, 27
long-term goals 19, 22, 24, 27

management of stress	.33
management of time	.29
managing performance	120
meetings	110
mental attitude	.15
meta-message	51-52, 58
mirroring	.61
mission statement	.98
motivating	.75
motivation	75, 95, 135
negative self-perceptions	.14, 24
negotiation	67-69, 70, 71, 72, 75, 135
networks	.10, 98
non-verbal	.58
non-verbal communication	.51, 58, 62
obituary	.21, 22
objective criteria	.71-72
office automation	112
open door policy	112
open positions	.60
open-ended questions	.79
options	.71
passive behaviour	.38
peers	9
performance	8-9, 104, 115, 121-122, 127, 132-133
performance appraisal	103, 120-122
planning	6, 19, 96
posture	.59, 61
power	10, 13, 28, 38, 46, 72, 129, 131-132
powerlessness	.14
pride	96, 100
priorities	.17, 28, 30, 98
procrastination	.29, 31
productivity	132
quality control	135
questions	44, 70, 75-77, 82, 108-109
recognition	.99
reflective questions	43, 80-81
relationships	7, 65-66, 72, 131
responsibility	11, 15, 27, 29-30, 46, 85, 104, 128, 134

restructuring of work	135
retributive behaviour	38
rhetorical questions	81
risk	6, 8, 19, 38, 45, 77-78, 100, 118, 132, 135
roles	19-20
seeking feedback	118
self-esteem	9, 100
semi-autonomous groups	131
service	98, 103
short-term goals	23-24, 27
shyness	42
skills	9, 38, 136
speeches	111
stress	33-35
submissive behaviour	38, 45
subordinates	10
subordinates' subordinates	10
success	6, 7, 10-11, 16, 129, 134
teams	131, 133
teleconferencing	109
telephone	108
time	27-29, 126, 128, 133
training	98, 103, 110, 123-124, 135
trick questions	77
trust	69, 75, 87, 117, 132-134
turnover	43
unions	131, 133
values	10, 17, 24, 65, 103, 106
video	109-110
vision	96-100
voice	44, 52-55
written communications	111
yes - no questions	80